Snake and Custard only

DEDICATION

To our granddaughter – a little girl who has stolen our hearts and who brings
so much joy and happiness to our family.

Lily Emma Hardy-Wilkinson, this book is for you.

Designed and printed by
Cambrian Printers Ltd
Aberystwyth

FOREWORD BY WILLIAM HOBBS

About a month ago, I was walking up Emai Shan, a stunningly beautiful mountain in Si Chuan province, central China. I was joined along this gruelling climb by some good friends of mine who had been travelling with me for several months. Every so often we would stop when something caught our eye, usually a large colourful and often hairy caterpillar or a particularly large spider. We would stand and stare, take some close-up photos and wait for it to 'do' something, before continuing our climb. Sometimes, if we were lucky, we would spot a monkey or baboon wandering across our path. We reached our destination, an icy cold and slightly damp guest house, near the top of the mountain after dark and slumped ourselves down on the hard yet mercifully horizontal mattresses. It had been a killer climb and our legs felt like they needed a month to recover, but we had seen some of the most impressive views in all of China and so were keen to review all our scenic shots. We soon realised that the majority of our photos were the same. They were not of the incredible mountain views, but animals, lots and lots of photos of animals. My likeminded friends and I had snapped most of the bugs and critters on the mountain, and it was great. Their fascination for creatures matched my own... almost. We began exchanging stories about who had seen which type of snake, or shark or bat, and where or how and, of course, who had had the most dangerous encounter. We eventually got on to how each of us had become interested in animals, where the fascination began, and it became apparent that is was something we had each just 'loved since childhood'.

It was during this evening of exhaustion and story-telling that I recalled, to my friends, my memories of a tall bearded man. About how he had visited my school a couple of times to host animal evenings for the pupils and parents of my primary school. My memories are vivid, however after reading the account of one of these particular evenings here in this book, perhaps not entirely accurate (there is video evidence, I'm told). Over a cold beer, I described to my friends about how a skinny, slightly undersized kid sat himself right on the front row in our assembly hall as close as possible to the mysterious collection of large boxes with the breathing holes, trying desperately to see inside, wanting to jump up and open those boxes, to see, to touch and to hold whatever lay inside. I told them about how this child wowed the tall bearded man sweating under the hot lights, with his brilliant knowledge of animals. How he asked many clever and relevant questions on behalf of himself and everyone else present. Of course, that bright little lad was me and the fantastic tall bearded man was Mr Wilkinson. I remembered learning so much, like how snakes are not slimy at all and about owls and their pellets and their incredible revolving heads, about chinchillas sand baths and red-kneed tarantulas itchy hairs. But above all this, I remember holding the snake. I loved it.

Facts are essential. Facts like how long a creature lives, how big it gets, how many babies it has, where it comes from, and what it eats. These kinds of facts are very very important. However, having these facts presented to you whilst the animal in question is clinging to your arm with its huge talons or wrapping its cool scaly skin around your shoulders blows any biology lesson taken before or since, right out of the water.

I was told an unusual thing when I was asked to write this foreword. Apparently I came to Mr Wilkinson in a dream, or more accurately, the inspiration to ask me to pen this foreword came from him having a dream / nightmare about me. The strange thing is that the dream occurred around the very same time I was retelling my account of the animal evenings to my friends. I had not really talked about it with anyone for years, but that evening with my friends the memories seemed to pop up from nowhere, and it felt great to reminisce. A bizarre coincidence perhaps. Chance or serendipity, who can say? The fact that I still haunt this man is worrying. Nevertheless, I am honoured to have been asked to do this. I can also steal this opportunity and apologise for putting Mr Wilkinson through such a harrowing night, for any disruption or stress I might have caused through my persistence to have every single one of my questions answered. I also want to say thanks, a very big thanks, because they were great evenings that have had a lasting impression on me. Enjoy the book.

William the Tormentor (or just 'Will' to my mates)
17 November 2006

ACKNOWLEDGEMENTS

I would like to thank the following people for their help in the compilation of this book.

Firstly, to my daughter Emma, who, despite being in the final weeks of pregnancy, proof-read and deciphered my hand-written scrawl, before tirelessly typing it all up and formatting it on the computer.

To Emma's other half, Robert Hardy, who kindly offered his artistic talents, the results of which can be seen in his amusing illustrations throughout the book.

To number one son Toby, and his other half Siân, for reading through the completed stories and laughing at all the right moments, which was most encouraging.

To my mother-in-law, Alice 'Lallie' Williams, a seamstress of unparalleled talent, who, overcoming her phobia of snakes, made my very first snake carrying bag.

To Gaye Groves, who had the unenviable task of being the first person to have to make both head and tail of my first attempts at this book, and for her unstinting patience and advice in helping me to arrive at an acceptable format.

To Pam Musto, who, with my wife Val, co-wrote the hilarious poem, 'Ode to a Parrot'.

A very special mention, plus many many thanks must go to William – now known as Will – Hobbs, undoubtedly the star of one of my stories, who has very kindly agreed to write the foreword.

The last time I saw Will, or rather his hand continually waving annoyingly in front of me, was twenty years ago when he was just six years old and I was giving an evening talk at his school, then known as Kinnerton CP.

Not surprisingly, after twenty years, Will proved difficult to track down, and it was only with the help of his mum (thanks Pauline) that we eventually found him, teaching English to schoolchildren in China.

I therefore sincerely hope that history is going to be repeated, and that amongst Will's pupils is a little six year old Chinese boy who will make William suffer as I did on that 'Evening with William Hobbs'.

Finally, I would like to thank my own other (better) half, Val, for her faith in me and her continual encouragement to push on with this project during the many occasions when my brain was beginning to flag.

Thank you and God bless you all.

Stuart Wilkinson – November 2006

CONTENTS

INTRODUCTION

Inevitable: - Unavoidable, sure to happen, certain, necessary, sure, unpreventable.

When I looked up the word inevitable and its meanings in a dictionary, it made me realise that no-one's life is unplanned. Right from the beginning, sets of circumstances come together to shape one's future and that fact, dear readers in inevitable.

My father and his father before him, were nature lovers though neither was averse to taking advantage of nature for their own ends so to speak. My grandfather had a little brook running literally through his back garden, between the rows of potatoes, cabbages and peas, and whilst tending his vegetable plot it was inevitable that he would often espy a fine brown trout that would no doubt complement the wonderful vegetables later that day at dinner.

During the summer months when the evenings were light and long, my father, myself and a large pram containing my baby brother would set out for an almost nightly walk along the country lanes near our home. I was about four or five years old at the time and enjoyed these walks immensely even though my little legs would ache and I wished I could be lifted up on to the pram. This was unthinkable, for a reason which I shall now relate. My father would at times need to gain access to the false floor of the pram, beneath which Neil, my baby brother would be peacefully sleeping, before being rudely tipped almost on his head as the false floor was lifted up and a miniature folding .22 rifle was produced. Within seconds of the loud crack of the rifle and little Neil once again being unceremoniously tipped onto his head, the rifle, now accompanied by a fine cock pheasant, a woodpigeon or maybe a rabbit was once again hidden safely away.

That all happened in about 1951. Now, fifty years later, could one imagine the uproar in the press at such a thing happening today?

I think that overall, the most important thing that made the inevitable even more inevitable was Miss Roberts, my very first teacher. It was she who 'fine tuned' what was already set up and working in my brain; who unwittingly set me on the path towards a life where nature would be my companion.
Probably only in her early twenties when she took up her first teaching post at my little school, I couldn't have realised then, that she would shape my life in the world of nature.

Miss Roberts was really into all things wild and wonderful and it was only a day or two into my school life before I too was under the same wonderful spell that had itself controlled her life.

One of the first things that she did was to start a nature table – something which I had never heard of. Unlike many nature tables I have seen since, this one changed with the seasons, such as the first snowdrops of spring, I can see them now, five pure white bowed-headed flowers in a ceramic inkwell filled with water, then a few weeks later came the sticky buds of the horse chestnut and the catkins of the hazel and pussy willow. Then there were birds nests of all shapes and sizes and even birds eggs usually in the form of hatched out shells, and then when summer finally arrived there would be the caterpillars and cocoons of the many different types of moth and butterfly.

It was whilst in Miss Roberts' class that I first saw frog spawn and tadpoles and I would listen fascinated as she related to us the life cycles of these creatures.

But it was the Autumn nature table that left its biggest impression on me, beautiful fallen leaves of red and gold with the musty smell of decay all about them, the ears of wheat, the acorns and conkers, hips and haws, I could go on and on. Even now fifty-odd years on, the smell of fallen leaves in the countryside brings back memories of Miss Roberts' Autumn nature table.

It was a sad day when I moved up from Miss Roberts' class to make way for new children beginning their school lives and I always envied these new starters, knowing what a wonderful year they had ahead of them.

I eventually left the little school and moved up to the new 'Big School' and pretty-well lost contact with Miss Roberts, although most mornings as I waited for my school bus to take me to my new school, I would see Miss Roberts struggling under the weight of her brown leather Gladstone bag, and I would try to imagine what goodies lay therein, a birds nest or two, acorns, conkers or maybe a preserving jar containing frogspawn.

Miss Roberts herself eventually moved on to a larger school and it would be many years before I would see her again. In fact it would be fifty years before our paths crossed again quite literally. I was driving up our narrow lane one afternoon when I became aware of a figure heading down the lane toward me, a very frail-looking figure whose legs now required the assistance of a walking frame.

Miss Roberts as I remember her had been a pretty, petite little lady with short, dark wavy hair and a lovely smile, but what I remember more vividly was the quick steps she took when she walked. Now fifty years on, I again recognised these features, though the steps were now laboured, and I could not be certain that it was her and it was only when I slowed the car in order to let her struggle past me on her walking frame, she looked at me and gave me a lovely – instantly recognisable smile as a thank you for letting her pass, that I knew it was without doubt, her.

For the life of me, I cannot work out why, there and then I did not stop the car to speak to her, but I resolved that at a later date I would take the opportunity to talk about old times.

I did discover from other sources that she had married very late in life and had been living literally a stone's throw from Val and I, but then through illness, becoming a resident at a local nursing home from which she would, with the aid of her walking aid make regular visits to her home.

Sadly, a couple of weeks after seeing her, I read her obituary in our local paper and I regretted that I hadn't taken the opportunity to speak to her when I'd had the chance, to tell her how very grateful I was to her for that first wonderful year in school and how it had led to a lifelong love of nature. This love of nature has led me into many interesting situations and eventually into a career where, in spite of the age-old adage – never work with children or animals, I did both, together for many years!

My work took me into hundreds of schools in the North West, and involved lecturing to children of all ages on different classes of animals and always illustrating my talks with live creatures. The following chapters tell of many fascinating, funny and sometimes unbelievable stories of things that have happened over the years which still bring a smile to my face or a lump to my throat, when I recall them, and which I hope you will also find amusing, as I'm sure you inevitably will.

POUCHED APRICOTS AND CUSTARD ONLY

As mentioned in my previous chapter, I began school in 1951 at the age of four, and although the war had been over a few years, there were many items of food that were still on ration, and I can still remember my mother handing over ration books at our local store in exchange for goods.

Consequently waste was frowned upon and we kids were brought up to believe that even if you didn't like something, you mustn't waste it and it must be eaten. I suspect now that I became conditioned very early in life to abhor waste of any kind and I'm still like that today. On the rare occasions that I have to leave food either because I don't like it (which is rare) or because I have eaten sufficient, I still feel very guilty about leaving it on the plate.

Which brings me to school dinners. Love `em or hate `em, they were always available to those of us who did enjoy them, and I can walk into a school even now and the smells of school dinners, percolating through the corridors brings on a certain nostalgia which is hard to explain.

The only down side to school meals, at least where I was concerned, were the puddings now known as sweets. I enjoyed semolina believe it or not, but detested fruit in any form, not that there was much variety of fruit from which to choose.

One day each week our pudding consisted of sponge cake and custard and this was enjoyed by all the diners, so much so that if there were ever any seconds available there would be much clamouring for more.

Very often though after these seconds had been dished out there was only custard left and one of the dinner ladies known affectionately as Auntie Betty would shout out 'Custard only! Custard only!', and it became a joke in our family which exists to this day. When, on being collected from school by my mother she asked me what I'd had for school dinner, my reply was chips and tomatoes, followed by cake and custard only. I really believed (as four-year olds do) that the yellow stuff which covered the cake was called 'custard only.'

But as puddings go, the one that struck fear into me was stewed apricots and custard (only?). I detested apricots mainly because in those days sugar was in short supply and so such things as apricots tasted very tart.

But because I had been conditioned not to waste food I ate it. Well, sort of anyway. I would start by spooning every last drop of custard into my mouth – leaving the apricots until the very last, and then, trying not to heave, I would put them into my mouth and like a pre-hibernation dormouse would pouch them in my cheek. Dinnertime over, I would then go back into class, hoping that the teacher didn't ask me any questions and as far as I can remember, she never did.

Now, pouching stewed apricots for three hours is not something I would recommend, mainly because the acid in the fruit starts to eat away at the mucus lining of ones cheek, resulting in – ruddy great ulcers. At the end of the day I had to walk with my Mum for about a mile before reaching home, and I, complete with my apricot filled, ulcerated cheek pouch would, at around half way home, race on ahead knowing full well that to my left there was a little bridge over a stream in a field gateway, and I judged that if I could get far enough ahead of my mother without her seeing me, I could do a rapid left turn into the gateway, and by standing on the bridge rails, I could spit out that which had been eating away at my cheek lining all afternoon, into the fast flowing stream below.

It would take a few days for my secret ulcers to clear up, and before I knew it the next dose of apricots and custard only would come along.

A MOORHEN RECOVERS

We Brits are well known as bird lovers. Some of us keep birds, others are happy to just watch birds, others feed birds, becoming quite expert at who eats what, or who prefers black sunflower seeds and who would rather have the white or striped versions.

Some people are so keen on birds that they treat them like pets or even like their own children.

This was the case one Saturday afternoon when I answered the telephone to a very worried man. He and his wife live on a busy main road although the back of the house overlooks a marshy area which lies alongside the river Alyn.

Seemingly, the couple had a family of moorhens in the back garden. These birds raised their brood in the marshy ground but brought their chicks daily to the house for scraps and titbits with the effect that over the years, the birds had become very tame and confiding.

Then one day the gentleman of the house discovered the cock bird badly injured on the road in front of the house, presumably having been in a collision with a car.

The man took the bird into the house and asked his wife to tend the bird whilst he telephoned me.

I arrived at the house to find the lady in tears, stroking the badly injured bird and when I told them both that I would take the bird and do what I could for it, tears from both parties made me realise just how devoted they both were to their birds.

As I left with the bird I promised to bring it back to them when it had recovered. The lady's last words to me were 'Please don't let her die'.

Normally if I think a bird will die I will tell the person who brought it in as much, although if a child brings in a bird I will tell the child that I'll do my best for the animal, knowing full well that it will not survive.

So it was with these two lovely people. I left their home with an injured bird which I had as good as promised would survive when I knew that it would be dead before I got it home.

My fears for the bird's life were realised when I got home and discovered on opening the box that the bird had expired.

I now had a problem, two people were relying on me to return their 'pet' moorhen, I had told them I would do so, but obviously now this was impossible.

I had told the couple that it would be many weeks before the moorhen would be well enough to be released and so for a while at least I could keep up the pretence that it was still alive and slowly recovering.

About two months later I was out hawking rabbits with Heidi my Harris Hawk when Heidi spotted something in an adjoining field and flew over to investigate. As I followed her into the next field, I disturbed a moorhen from the bottom of the hedgerow and as the bird flew across the field towards a small pond, Heidi spotted it, took off from her perch in an ash tree and did a rather clever somersault, grabbing the moorhen as she did so.

Now as luck would have it Heidi had not harmed the moorhen and was only holding it by its main wing feathers, and so I gently took hold of the bird, whilst at the same time offering Heidi a reward in the form of a rabbit leg. She let go of the moorhen and I popped it into my hawking bag.

I would normally have released the bird straight away, but a plan had formed in my mind.

The following morning saw me knocking on the door of the couple's house, there were more tears as they inspected the now 'recovered' moorhen, and I myself had a lump in my throat as I watched the bird 'return' to its family in the reed bed.

HOW TO IDENTIFY A MERLIN – IN ONE SWIFT LESSON

'Is that Mr Wilkinson?', enquired the gruff sounding female voice at the other end of the telephone. 'I've got a merlin for you if you want it, it's the pet shop in town'. I was somewhat surprised at the call, as it's not every day that someone asks if you want a merlin; in fact it's a pretty rare occurrence I would have thought.

Very often, folk tend to mix up some of the smaller birds of prey and so I thought that the likelihood of its being a merlin was practically nil, and much more likely to be a kestrel or even a sparrowhawk.

'Are you sure it's a merlin?', was my first question. The indignant gruff voice in reply made me regret even thinking of contradicting her.

'I know my birds, it's most definitely a merlin. I should know because when I was a little girl a merlin attacked me'. Hmm, what with I thought, a baseball bat? Now merlins may be carnivorous birds of prey but attack humans they certainly do not. I continued to quiz the lady in order to establish just what the bird was.

'What colour is it?' I enquired, again being made to regret asking. 'Have you never seen a merlin before?' she said. 'You must know what colour they are!'. 'Yes I do', I replied 'but I'm asking you to tell me'. Silence for thirty seconds or so. 'Are you going to come over and collect it or shall I take it to the RSPCA?'. 'Yes I'll come over', I said. 'I just need to be sure what it is so that I can arrange some suitable food ready for it'. 'I've told you', came the bossy gruff lady again. 'It's a merlin. I should know, I've been attacked by one before, it's in a budgie cage'. The words 'budgie cage' sent me into panic mode, as a merlin in a budgie cage would wreck its feathers very quickly.

So after obtaining directions from the bossy sounding lady, I set off for her pet shop in a nearby town. On entering the shop I was met by a rather stout looking lady of about sixty years of age with dyed black hair and vivid red lipstick.

I introduced myself and enquired about the merlin at which point the lady immediately started telling me of when she was a little girl and a merlin had attacked her. I asked how she knew she'd been attacked by a merlin and not some other bird of prey. 'My mother told me', she said. 'My mother knew all about birds, she knew what she was talking about'.

I could see that the conversation was taking on the quality of a halfpenny book and so I asked to see the merlin. With that the lady removed a pink towel which had been draped over a blue and chrome budgie cage in one corner of the shop. 'There you go', said the black haired red-lipped bird expert. 'One merlin'.

I peered into the cage, and there it was lying before me with its beautiful big eyes blinking at me and its beautiful dark plumage with not a feather out of place. Then there were the wings, those long slim sickle wings to give the bird speed in order to pursue and catch its prey.

'Now do you believe me?', said the lady. 'I told you it was a merlin didn't I? I should know, when I was a little girl I was....'. 'Yes', I said, 'you were attacked by a merlin you say. Did it look like this one?'. 'Of course', she said. 'I know my birds'.

I carefully lifted the bird out of the cage, checked it over and then took it outside and threw it into the air where it quickly joined the other swifts as they screeched noisily around the town.

MISS ELLIE THE BULLFROG

The slip of pink paper that fluttered through our letterbox one morning stated that there was, at our local post office, a parcel awaiting collection. Those were the days before the private parcel delivery firms came onto the scene, and to my way of thinking, the post office delivery service was far more reliable than the modern equivalents.

For one thing, you would get your parcel at the same time as your other mail, first thing in the morning. Whereas the modern firms may deliver at any time of the day, when one was least likely to be at home.

Anyway, Val popped round to the post office to collect the parcel which contained either a Giant American Bullfrog or a Mexican Red- Kneed Tarantula. I say either, because the box bore no indication as to what creature lurked within its walls.

By the weight of the box, Val deduced that it was the bullfrog that had been held for collection and then proceeded to tell Mr Ledgard the Postmaster to look out for another parcel arriving within a day or two – this parcel would contain the big tarantula.

On learning that he had been holding a parcel containing a giant frog, Mr Ledgard, obviously unsettled by this fact, nervously stammered out that he didn't like 'ffrogs'. Mr Ledgard on hearing that within the next twenty-four hours he would be sharing the small space behind the Post Office counter with a tarantula was visibly shaking and Val feared for his welfare.

The following morning brought an early telephone call from Mr Ledgard who deciding that the standard GPO pink slip would on this occasion cause an unnecessary delay, had decided that a phone call to us, with the promise that he would open the shop early if we would, 'Come over now please and collect this spider. Please I don't like spiders!'.

Val dashed over to the Post Office immediately, and as promised, the shop door was open early. A heavily perspiring Mr Ledgard was standing outside at the front of the shop and without so much as a good morning, he pointed through the open doorway and said, 'It's in there on the counter, go in and get it will you, I don't like spiders!'. Val walked in and picked up the box and bade good morning to a now much calmer Mr Ledgard.

Anyway, back to the bullfrog. Taking the fairly heavy box into the house, we proceeded to open it, and with the flaps of the lid now folded back, we observed a thick polythene bag which had been inflated with air to keep the creature alive. We lifted the bag from the confines of the box and looked through the clear sides. We observed a small amount of water and a large amount of sphagnum moss, presumably to prevent the frog from drying out.

The bag had been tightly knotted and so I carried it through to the lounge where I knew there to be a pair of scissors as it would be much simpler to cut into the bag rather than fiddle with a knot that looked as if it would never yield.

With the bag on the floor, I cut into the thick polythene wall of the bag, a slight hiss of escaping air told me we were through. It now only remained for me to make the cut larger in order that I could get my hands inside to extricate an amphibian which I had not yet actually seen due to the large amount of moss which obliterated much of the inside of the bag.

Putting my hand into the bag, I removed the large bunch of moss and as I did so, I became aware that the large olive coloured mass that remained within the bag was a big bullfrog. In fact it wasn't just big, it was a monster, two pale gold coloured eyes studied me without blinking. The large bag of skin where the chin should be, pulsed up and down with a regular rhythm alternating with the in and out movements of the creature's sides as it breathed in the fresh air.

Although she was an awesome sight, she looked fairly calm and so, placing my hands around her sides, I gently lifted her from the now deflated bag at which point Val moved rather quickly to the far end of the lounge some six or eight metres away.

Once clear of the bag, we could appreciate just how big the frog was and it was the legs that made us realise just what a powerful creature we were dealing with. These rear limbs reminded one of the 'drumsticks' of a turkey, packed with muscle that once powered up, would propel the green monster into the next room – which is exactly what did happen. The fact that Val and I had begun talking excitedly, obviously made the frog a little uneasy and with an almighty push of the huge green drumsticks, the big frog was airborne.

Our lounge was once two rooms which had eventually been knocked into one resulting in one very superior long-jump course for an Olympic standard amphibian.

Val was kneeling at the far end of the lounge facing me and had seen the frog catapulting itself toward her, but could do nothing to prevent the frog from hitting her full in the chest, knocking her backwards as it did so. We actually thought that Val may have cracked a rib in the accident, such was the force of the impact and for many days afterwards the impact site was sore and tender.

The giant frog was eventually installed in a large vivarium where she lived for many years, making almost daily trips to schools far and wide where she impressed many children with her size, and horrified many more when they were told that her favourite food was dead mice which she swallowed whole. The dead mouse swallowing process was ably assisted by her own eye-balls which would descend through the roof of her mouth, acting like some primitive pushing tool to lever the mouse down the throat.

At the time that we acquired her there was an immensely popular television drama called 'Dallas' being screened on a weekly basis, and it seemed that the whole of the UK was hooked. One of the characters, the matriarch of the family in the production was called by her husband, 'Miss Ellie', and as our big female American Bullfrog reminded us of Miss Ellie, then we decided that we should call her just that.

HORATIO

Horatio was a European Eagle Owl, which a friend had kindly obtained for me to use in my school talks. He was about three months old when he came to me and was almost completely full feathered, although he did have two very comical looking pom poms of thick white down on the top of his head at the point where his ear tufts would eventually sprout.

He had been handled from birth and was exceptionally tame and good tempered which was just as well, because a bad tempered eagle owl can be quite a handful.

The Latin name for the European Eagle Owl is Bubo Bubo and I often wondered whether they were given this name after the call, which they make, which basically goes 'Boo Boo Boo Boo'.

Because of his impressive size and huge wingspan of nearly two metres, he was probably one of the most popular of all my school 'props.' I even taught him to 'Boo Boo' to order, and I only had to quietly whisper 'Boo Boo' and he, proudly pushing his white throat feathers forward loudly repeated the sound.

Another trick I taught him was to open his wings on command. With him sitting on my fist I would say, 'Open your wings Horatio'. Of course he never did and so I would look for a child in the audience that was maybe wearing something unusual. I would say, 'Horatio will only do things for someone wearing a pink hair band', and I would point to the child I had selected and ask her to come up and help me.

I would again ask the owl to open his wings and again he would refuse, so I would then ask the little girl to ask him. The child would ask the question but invariably omit the word PLEASE. So I would ask her to repeat the question making sure she used the word PLEASE. As she did so I would rock my arm back and forth, so discreetly that it would go unnoticed to the audience, but would have the effect of unbalancing the large bird on my fist, who, in order to regain his balance would open his wings wide.

The trick always went down well with the audience and I remember one teacher asking me how long it had taken to teach the trick to Horatio, so I must have been convincing!

When he was about three years old, Horatio became sexually mature and because he was humanised or imprinted, he now saw humans as being suitable mating prospects which, though sounding quite amusing can be a big problem.

So for about three months from December to March or April, Horatio had nookie on his mind, which caused much embarrassment.

He would, in his efforts to have his wicked way with me, try to get upon my head in order to mate. So having to think of a solution rather quickly, I decided to let Val handle him and thereby reduce his contact with me.

It worked...for about forty-eight hours and then he started to become amorous to Val, who, always having an answer to every problem, took to wearing a tweed hat when handling him, which although it didn't prevent his advances, certainly did prevent a badly lacerated scalp. Horatio absolutely adored the hat and we realised that we now had an owl with a hat fetish, which we just had to put a stop to.

The only answer was to build an aviary with enclosed walls which prevented him from seeing out and seeing us and allowing him the company of a very sexy looking female Eagle Owl, who being much larger than he would almost certainly 'sort him out.'

Sadly this ruse failed and whenever he heard us in the garden, we could hear him 'boo boo-ing' to us from the aviary, whilst at the same time scraping a nest in the corner of the aviary.

What we didn't realise was that as he scraped a nest site, he was digging down beneath the foundation of the aviary, and it was only when seeing the hole on the outside of the aviary one morning that we realised he'd dug his way out.

This was a really worrying run of events, as we had one very randy eagle owl living somewhere amongst the woodland at the back of our home who would be watching our every move to silently glide down onto our heads in order to relieve his pent-up passion.

It would be even more dangerous at night because we wouldn't be able to see him, whereas he would be able to see us as clear as day. We became afraid to go out after dark, though nothing ever did happen, in fact we never saw Horatio again.

A few months later we had a call from the police in Greater Manchester saying that a large owl, fitting the description of Horatio was terrorising little old ladies in a park in Bolton, and would we come over to 'sort him out' please.

It seemed that Horatio had settled in the park, which had a good supply of food in the form of rabbits and squirrels and that he was quite happy. The trouble was, each morning at first light, elderly female senior citizens would leave the safety of their homes in order to take their little dogs for an early morning jolly. Many of these ladies would wear hats, and that's where the problem lay.

Horatio with his fetish for hats thought that he was being give the 'come on' by these ladies and would swoop down on them, with the ladies wrongly assuming that he was after their little dogs.

So off we went to Bolton armed with a large box, a strong glove and a tweed hat, but we were too late. A little old lady had retaliated and killed poor Horatio, probably with her Zimmer frame!

SETTING THE CAT AMONGST THE MERLINS – MARY BETH

Tim, a young falconer friend telephoned me early one Sunday morning. This was unusual, as Tim used to be (in his younger days) one of those people who were bored with Sundays and whose philosophy in life was to sleep through as much of the Holy Day as possible; wake up for a Sunday roast and then return to bed for the rest of the day. So for Tim to ring on a Sunday morning at 9.45am was most definitely out of character. 'Hiya Mr Wilkinson. Nicky has just found an injured merlin in the Quay (Connah's Quay) and wants to know if you want it'.

Two hours later, the lads were at my door with the injured bird, a beautiful little female merlin with a droopy wing but otherwise ok. That afternoon I took her to my local vet in order that he could check her over although I knew that the broken wing was her only problem. No disrespect to the veterinary world, but at the time of the incident very few vets treated wild creatures, especially birds of prey. So at the time there was absolutely no doubt in my mind that my own diagnosis was 100% accurate. I used to have to tell the vets what was wrong with some of the creatures I took to them (and still do in some cases) so I wasn't surprised when the vet told me that the bird did indeed have a broken wing and because of the delicate size of the merlin he was unable to fix the wing.

At the time the merlin was brought in I already had a male or 'Jack'merlin, another casualty, who had been found shot on the isle of Bute and had eventually found his way through different people to me. So we now had a pair and the least we could do was to put them together and hope that they would eventually breed.

The female had been wearing a British Trust for Ornithology (B.T.O.) ring when she was picked up and so I sent details from the ring to the B.T.O. and eagerly awaited their reply.

When the notes from the B.T.O. finally arrived back, I was astonished to discover that this little merlin had been ringed at a nest some eleven years before. Not as a baby but as a breeding bird. She was found to be so tame that she could be lifted from the nest and stroked etc etc and from what I could gather, she was quite a famous, much photographed bird. To cut a very long story short she got along famously with her new mate and did in fact produce infertile eggs a couple of years later, but old age rapidly overtook her and I found her dead in the aviary one morning. Two weeks later her mate also died, he was about ten years old which was quite a good age for a merlin.

I normally bury or burn deceased creatures but these two pretty little birds were in such good condition, the female was famous in that every photograph of a merlin one saw in bird books was of her. One could even read the numbers on her ring on many photographs. So the decision to ask a taxidermist friend to preserve them forever was not a difficult one and the birds were duly handed over.

Some weeks later I was met by my wife when I returned home from work who said excitedly 'Ron's been with the merlins, you'll love them, they're in the lounge'.

As I opened the door into the lounge Mary Beth our Siamese cat very very proudly walked out (as Siamese cats do) with that look on her face that says, 'I've sorted those two birds out for you. You know the ones on the coffee table next to your chair'. I almost cried when I saw my two beautiful little merlins, or what remained of them, thousands of feathers spread around the room, stuffing everywhere, a leg here, a beak there. If I get hold of that flamin' cat it will be a tail here, a paw there etc etc.

Whilst on the subject of Mary Beth and her disgusting habits, there is another story I must tell you. At the end of spring term at Val's school, temporary homes had to be found for the school pets, things like guinea pigs, gerbils, fish and also a pair of beautiful geckoes – small green spotted lizards with huge eyes and sucker feet.

Val had volunteered me to look after the geckoes as I had a spare vivarium in which to house them, and so she brought them home in a box and left them on the central heating boiler until I came home from work, when I could install them in their temporary home.

A short time later Val became aware of a crunching noise coming from the kitchen. Yes, you've guessed it. Mary Beth had decided to help herself to the geckoes, which took some explaining to the pupils when school resumed.

Mary Beth was a sort of rescue cat. She and her brother William had been owned by a local family, but when the husband was offered a job in Algeria which he accepted, it became obvious that they couldn't take their two Siamese cats with them. The problem was that no-one would re-home two cats and when we heard about them, the family was considering having them put to sleep. Val is rather soft where cats are concerned, and with a great deal of arm-twisting by Val, I too softened somewhat and agreed we should take them.

William, Mary Beth's brother was probably the worst thief one could ever imagine, although he rarely stole from us. Sundays seemed to be his favourite klepto days, and from about 9am onwards, William would often appear with a rasher of bacon or a string of sausages still hot from the pan, but from whom he was acquiring them we didn't find out for a few weeks. Then one Sunday morning I was near our front gate, when I heard shouting and cursing and on looking towards the source of the commotion, observed William exiting the kitchen window of our next-door-but-one neighbours, with a small joint of beef in his teeth. Obviously the lady of the house had put it out to cool and William had decided that he'd quite like the piece himself. How William didn't burn his mouth we'll never know, but he must have done, because he eventually stopped stealing freshly cooked food – or maybe he just decided to reform. Both William and Mary Beth are long deceased but (sadly) their genes live on in some of our other cats, all of which are much loved little characters. All of these descendants are cross breeds and all except two are black and white; the two exceptions are both Siamese lookalikes and have an uncanny resemblance to Mary Beth.

19

THE THINGS KIDS SAY

It's amazing some of the things kids come out with, sometimes saying something that they believe to be right but getting it only partially right.

Most of my school talks consisted of annual visits, sometimes one would do twice-yearly visits and it was one of these visits that prompted my next tale.

On a second visit to a school I always made a point of asking the children if they could remember what creatures they had seen on my previous visit. Most children would shoot their hands up and would be able to name at least one of the creatures correctly, though one little six year old I think, got her words mixed up. The children had correctly given three creatures from my last visit and the fourth creature, a very large green African Numbskull Toad was the only one that no-one had mentioned. No-one that is, until the little six year old lady, desperately waving her arm in the air trying to attract my attention, who, when asked what the last exhibit was, replied 'A big slimy green turd'.

A young lad from Liverpool (where else?) on hearing that the word NOCTURNAL, means to come out at night, I suppose, reasoned quite correctly when he said that his Nan had nocturnal teeth!

And finally, a little lad who most definitely got it right at four years old. I was talking to a class of eleven year olds who had in their midst a little four year old, a brother of one of the older children who because his class had finished early, was allowed to come into the talk whilst waiting for his sister.

My question to the class was, 'What was the name of the first fossilized bird?'. I looked at the faces before me hoping a hand would shoot up with an answer, but nothing materialised, and then I saw it, struggling to make it seen above the shoulders of the much older, bigger children in front of it. I could now see that it was the wee four year old that was trying to gain my attention and as no-one else was attempting an answer, I thought he may come up with an amusing reply. I repeated my question, at the same time pointing towards the little boy, his reply stunned me. 'Archaeopteryx Sir!!'.

HOW MANY B'S IN THAT? (PPPICK UP A PPASTERN)

For many years we kept a very old donkey called Lucy and a Section A pony called Izzy who spent their days grazing on our fields. Every so often we would have to call in a farrier to trim their hooves that seemed to grow at an alarming rate. Neither of these animals had ever worn shoes so it was just a case of trimming at regular intervals, even though both the donkey and the pony really detested the farrier; mainly because he was rough with them, he was also rather loud, banging his tool box around and really doing nothing that would give the poor nags confidence.

On top of all this, the poor man had a very bad stammer which I think most people would try to ignore.

One day we had visitors, a friend of Val's and her precocious little daughter who was if I remember correctly, about six or seven years old at the time. During the afternoon the farrier arrived to trim the feet of the nags and of course the little girl had to get involved; helping to round up the nervous pair, bringing them down to solid ground and holding them steady whilst the farrier went about his work.

The farrier could see that the little girl was interested in the proceedings and in all fairness to him he did his best to explain the different parts of the equine foot, such as the hoof and the frog. It was when he came to another part of the leg that things became embarrassing. 'And this', he said, 'is the pastern bbbbbbone'. With that, the precocious little child was heard to exclaim, 'Good heavens man! How many b's were in that!?'.

PHOBIAS

The lady on the other end of the telephone introduced herself as a reporter for one of our local newspapers. It transpired that this young lady had, for as far back as she could remember, a snake phobia, and her editor, knowing of this phobia thought it would make good reading if this young reporter could visit my home, with the intention of overcoming her fear of these reptiles. Not wishing to appear overly sadistic, I agreed and a date was set for the interview.

Two days later I answered the door to two representatives of the said newspaper, Debbie, the young lady reporter whom I guessed to be in her late twenties and her photographer, a young man of a similar age whose name was Geoff.

After a coffee and a chat in which I outlined what we were going to see and do, Geoff unpacked his camera and we were ready to start. During coffee I had shown pictures of various types of snake to the couple in order to prepare them for the real thing. I fully understood that Debbie was absolutely terrified of snakes, what I hadn't bargained for was that Geoff was also non too keen on the things.

I had brought into the room two bags, one small, about the size of a pillowcase, the other a very large hessian sack held an obviously much larger beast.

The small bag was untied and placed on my knee and after a minute or so, the contents, in the form of a one metre long American corn snake, began to creep out of the bag and on to my arm. At this point all the handling was done by myself whilst the young lady observed and the photographer clicked away from the safety of the settee opposite.

Now everyone who has a fear of snakes, believes them to be wet and slimy, which is understandable as the scales are almost always shiny in order to catch sunlight which in turn warms up the cold-blooded snake.

Watching me handling the snake seemed to relax the young lady who asked lots of questions, jotting down her notes in shorthand with only a slightly noticeable shake of the pen.

Within half an hour or so, Debbie had progressed from observing to touching and then to handling, the snake loving every minute of the proceedings. Corn snakes are very endearing little snakes and love human contact, and this little fellow was no exception. Debbie persuaded Geoff to have a go and he too seemed to enjoy the experience.

After about an hour I suggested that we might now move on to the large bag and Debbie and Geoff, full or their new found knowledge and experience, agreed.

With the corn snake back in the bag, the sack was then untied and as before, the much larger snake proceeded to exit the bag, and at approximately four metres in length with a head the size of a man's hand and a very large girth, the Burmese python looked impressive.

Again, I allowed the couple to watch me stroking the snake before they too were stroking it, just as they had the corn snake. Everything was going to plan, that is, until the telephone rang and with it being in the adjoining room, I had to leave the couple alone with the snake while I went to answer the call. As I entered the room to answer the phone, I inadvertently allowed Daisy, my wife's little cavalier spaniel out of the room where she had been put out of harm's way. She then sneaked into the room with Debbie, Geoff and a very large snake.

Shouting, screaming, growling and whining coming from the lounge forced me to cut short the telephone conversation and dash back to the lounge to see what all the fuss was about. The sight that met my eyes is one that I'll never forget. Debbie in her stiletto heels had climbed onto our lovely dining table, the snake was winding its way up one of the table legs towards her. Geoff was behind the settee, white-faced and uttering total gibberish, but of little Daisy there was no sign. My first thought was that the snake on seeing Daisy entering the room had assumed it was meal time, had eaten Daisy and was now about to make Debbie the main course, before devouring Geoff for pudding.

Putting the snake back into the bag, I rescued Geoff and between us we managed to lift Debbie down from her perch on the table. With that, little Daisy appeared from behind the curtain looking very sheepish for causing so much trouble.

I have never seen two people exit a house so fast in all my life. The pair didn't even thank me, though I hadn't expected them to. Two or three days later Debbie's article appeared in our local paper along with some lovely photos, although the article didn't mention the incident with Daisy.

PETA AND THE SNAKE

Another incident relating to snake phobias occurred in a school in Birkenhead. The headmaster had specifically asked for a snake to be included in the talk as a member of staff was snake phobic and he thought that seeing a tame snake would help her overcome her fear.

The school hall was typical of most schools built in the 1960's with a door at the far end with a round window. The idea was that the female teacher who's name was Peta would observe the snake from the window, and as she gained confidence, would eventually enter the hall and sit at the back, moving forward to other empty seats left specifically for her until she eventually found herself directly in front of me, just a metre or so from the snake.

This idea worked perfectly, with Peta getting closer and closer every few minutes until, as planned she was directly in front of myself and the snake which was wrapped unconcernedly around my neck.

The talk over, Peta was persuaded to stroke the snake, no more than that, as she felt that was sufficient and I didn't push the issue.

Peta then invited me back to the staff room for a cup of tea and I put the snake back into its box, and followed her and the other teachers to the staff room for a well-earned cuppa.

The topic of conversation was the snake and how Peta had so bravely dealt with her phobia and everyone commented on what a good idea it was from the headmaster, and I too felt quite pleased that this lady was no longer snake phobic. Then the staff room door burst open, in sprang the headmaster, who had removed his tie and threw it at Peta saying something about it being a snake. I laugh about it now, but I felt so sorry for the poor woman as I watched her shaking uncontrollably as she headed out of the school gate, and I often wonder if she ever went back.

SCURDY CAT

I have little doubt that in the world of rapid off-the-cuff comments, Merseysiders take some beating, and whether one is on the Birkenhead side or the Liverpool side of the once great river Mersey. The fact remains that as well as being genuine, enterprising and sometimes roguish, they are a comical lot.

During the last war, many Merseyside children were evacuated to Wales with the result that subsequent generations of Merseysiders consider Wales to be the 'promised land'.

Over twenty years ago, Val my wife, who was pregnant with Toby our son, was told by her gynaecologist at Wrexham, that she would have to sit out the remaining eight weeks of her pregnancy in the Oxford Street Maternity Hospital in Liverpool. Now eight weeks is a long time to spend in bed, even worse is the fact that Val was upset that she would be in a strange place with many strange faces and more importantly, she would be a long long way from our home in Wales.

The day following that which saw Val take to her hospital bed, now renamed 'Ossie' bed, I paid my first daily visit, half expecting Val to be really down in the dumps. But no, Val said that she was being treated like a celebrity with someone or other popping in every few minutes to see if she was ok and did she need anything.

We suspected that on Val's admission, the word had got around the maternity unit that there was a Welsh lady in one of the single rooms. This, to all the Liverpudlian staff, must have been the equivalent to the appearance of the Virgin Mary at Lourdes. A real Welsh lady sitting up in bed wearing a red cape, a tall black hat and sporting a hairy mole on her chin!! Val said that the staff, and especially the auxiliary staff kept on looking through her door and with typical 'scouse' endearment, enquiring "Yorite Queen?"

By far the most amusing incident which took place during one of my talks, involved a school in Bootle, a suburb of Liverpool. Most schools had subjects or projects each term, maybe on migration, hibernation, flight or whatever, and would ask me to gear my talk to whatever projects the class in particular was working on.

This particular school was doing various projects on fear and of course I was asked to bring along animals that are associated with fear.

One of my props was a very large, though docile, spider, a Mexican Red Kneed Tarantula to be precise. This creature was quite content to sit upon one's hand for as long as required to do so, she didn't walk much, she certainly didn't run, scuttle or jump, and yet the presence of this spider in a classroom had a strange effect on people. I've seen grown men scurry out of the room at the sight of this huge hairy creature, (and the spider) and most children become quite mesmerised by the sight.

The whole of Year Two in Bootle were silent. Silent that is, except for two young chaps who were totally engrossed in whispered conversation. This annoyed me somewhat and I broke off my talk to ask the two what was so important. One of the boys looked at me and exclaimed in thick scouse, 'We wus talking about feer seer. Me Da's a real scurdy cat, he's so scurd that when me mam goes to work at the ossie every night, he has to have Mrs Jones from next door to come and sleep with him, he's so scurd seer'.

ONE L OF AN APPRAUSE

Within the Welsh counties which I covered with my talks, were many tiny villages and hamlets with equally tiny schools. One in particular which I remember had only twelve pupils, all of differing ages, and who, had they been in an average sized village school would be in different classes to each other had, in this particular case, a distinct disadvantage educationally in that there were only two members of staff, one of whom was the headmaster. I cannot begin to work out how these pupils were taught.

Schools like the aforementioned would rarely reply to my information circulars, as they would be unable to afford my fees. I used to feel sorry for these little schools and would often negotiate a peppercorn fee or sometimes in the case of the above mentioned establishment, take no fee whatsoever, my reasoning being, that these small schools were regularly overlooked by their council authority for spending and so suffered anyway, often having to rely on the good will of the parents or even that of the small community itself for any small luxuries for the school.

Other schools had a system where, rather than the pupils missing out on treats such as those offered by myself, would join up for an hour or two with another small school within the county. In this way, the combined effort would often result in a total audience of fifty to eighty pupils.

I well remember making my way to one such school gathering in a tiny village in Denbighshire. It was an icy morning at the beginning of March and though the main roads had been cleared of snow a week or so before, the little countryside roads which led to the school some two miles from the main road, most definitely had not been cleared properly, having metre high banks of snow where a local farmer had used his tractor-mounted snow plough to enable the locals to go about their business as best they could.

So after leaving the main road, I followed the signs for the village where the school was situated. The narrow lanes that led into the hills were icy and needed much care and concentration if one didn't wish to end up as a statistic.

After some minutes of driving I became aware of a land rover in front of me, the back of which contained, in addition to a couple of border collie sheep dogs, half a dozen children, with two or three more in the front seat alongside the lady driver.

All along the route, other four-wheel drive vehicles joined us, forming a convoy; there was even a tractor pulling a trailer containing kids and dogs.

The village consisted of literally a couple of pretty little dwellings and at the far end of this one hundred metre long village stood the school, not much larger than an air-raid shelter, it was surrounded by scores of four wheel drive vehicles, tractors, unimogs, you name it.

It was then that I realised that the two schools which had joined up for my talk had been planning this amalgamation for months and rather than let the unexpected bad freeze up affect them, had organised local farmers to 'get the kids in or bust.'

Before I commenced my talk, I was introduced to the pupils and staff by the headmaster of the school which was hosting the event, and all in all there was a total of approximately thirty children and six adults; the sum total of the two village schools.

During the introduction, I became aware that the host headmaster was unable to pronounce the letter 'L' and I suppose that because Welsh was the predominant language in these areas that it wouldn't have caused the gentleman much of a problem normally.

The trouble was, when I had finished my talk, the headmaster gave a small speech of thanks in English which in itself went without a hitch, it was his final couple of sentences which made me chuckle.

'Now chirdren, how do we express our thanks? We crap don't we? But so as not to frighten the animars I want you arr to crap reearry quietry'.

Whenever I drive through that particular area I often try to visualise thirty kids and half a dozen teachers crapping in unison!

THE BILIOUS LITTLE BLACON BOY

Blacon is an overspill area for the combined areas of Chester and Ellesmere Port, being roughly midway between both. Like many overspills it has a large population and consequently has more than its fair share of schools, many of which I visited at one time or another.

One of these schools had booked a talk for a 9.15am start. Now I personally disliked these early starts because one would very often be interrupted by children coming in late.

This particular morning, I had already begun my talk when the door opened and in walked a very pale looking little boy accompanied by his mum. I stopped my talk fully expecting the little lad to take his place and his mum would leave the room. Instead, mother made a bee-line for me and without apology proceeded to tell me that her little Frankie, or whatever his name was, had not slept all night because he was so excited about my talk and seeing the animals, and would I keep an eye on him as he now seemed unwell. The little boy sat himself down on the floor behind his classmates and his mother made her way home.

I took out an American Bullfrog for my next prop and held her around the waist with her huge legs dangling in front of the children. As I did this, I noticed little Frankie was beginning to fidget unnaturally and I noticed that his face was now of a similar shade to that of the frog. Half a second later and the little lad had thrown up his last meal and by the looks of it, the previous one as well, all over the head and shoulders of the little girl in front of him. Before the second wave of vomit could hit her she made a quick exit out of the way, the offending regurgent hitting the floor where she had been sitting. A teacher, quick off the mark, ran over to little Frankie and motioned to him to leave the room via the small space in front of him. The stupid boy should have trod warily to avoid the slippery mess on the floor but in his rush to get out, he slipped, with his feet shooting forward, and falling onto his back, aquaplaned across the hall towards the exit.

The lad would be in his twenties now and at the last Winter Olympics I eagerly scanned the competition board for a Blacon boy called Frankie competing in the Luge.

THE HARE

One of my more interesting school assignments was to give talks to schoolchildren in Scotland's beautiful Dumfries and Galloway area. These talks would last four days in total and were organised for me by the daughter of one of Val's friends. Andrea, the daughter, herself a schoolteacher in one of the Scottish schools, had heard of my talks through her mum, Kath, and had thought what a good idea it would be if she could secure my services.

Andrea and her husband Richard, a Forestry Consultant had kindly offered to put me up for the duration of my visit, in exchange for a talk at the imminent birthday of their little boy Brian.

The tour went off perfectly and was enjoyed by pupils and staff of the many tiny Scottish schools within Dumfries and Galloway. I too thoroughly enjoyed the change of scenery and the varied wildlife of the area.

Now Andrea is a rather excellent cook and being married to a Forester, had an enviable access to game of many species, from the salmon of the River Cree which tumbled and roared outside their front door, to the wonderful wild venison from the roe and red deer which could often be observed feeding almost at their back door.

On completing my final talk on the Friday afternoon, Andrea and Richard invited me to join them for a final meal before I set off on the long journey back to Wales. The main course of this meal was a casserole of venison which was superbly cooked and presented, and which I have never forgotten.

The meal over, I bade my farewells to the family and began what was to be a four or five hour journey. Trouble was, I had, as usual eaten rather too much good food and I felt distinctly uncomfortable. The waistband on my trousers had become very tight and I couldn't envisage travelling very far in that condition. So what did I do? I stopped the car, undid my belt and unzipped my trousers which offered instant relief, and in this state I proceeded on my way across the desolate moors.

When I am driving at night I always keep a look out for things such as rabbits and hares which have been hit by cars, and if not too badly damaged, I will collect them, pop them into a bag and take them home to feed to my birds of prey, my dogs, cats, and even myself.

I had been travelling about half an hour when my headlights picked out the still, prostrate form of a mountain hare that had been in collision with a motor vehicle within the past few minutes. I stopped the car on the lonely road, leaving the headlights on to illuminate the hare in order that I could check it out, and if not too badly crushed it would go into my bag. I walked over to the hare and picking it up, held it aloft in the headlights. With that, a vehicle with lights blazing rounded a bend in the road, heading directly towards me; at the moment the driver applied his brakes to avoid hitting me, my unsecured trousers responding to the natural laws of gravity, unnaturally but suddenly dropped around my ankles.

Holding the hare in one hand and trying to pull up my trousers with the other I limped hurriedly back to the car and hastily sped off into the night. What the occupants of the other car had thought on seeing this astonishing sight I dread to think but about twenty minutes later a pair of headlights accompanied by a blue flashing light became worryingly apparent in my rear view mirror.

As the officer strolled over to the car, Newspaper headlines flashed before my eyes. One headline rather inappropriately claimed 'Local Naturalist Picked Up By The Fuzz.' This incident turned out to be unconnected to the episode with the hare. The constable had been rightfully investigating what he considered to be a suspicious looking vehicle carrying boxes. I explained where I was coming from, what I had been doing in Scotland and where I was now going, and ended up giving him a free wildlife talk at the side of the little moor land road in Scotland. And in case you are wondering, after the episode with the hare, had secured my trousers – and a good job too!

LITTLE OWLS UP THE CHIMNEY

For many years we have always been available to take in orphaned wildlife, the idea being to rehabilitate these birds as soon as possible back into the wild.

We were given three baby little owls by our local RSPCA inspector one day, and because they were able to feed themselves, though too young to fly, we thought they would be easy to eventually return to the wild.

I put them in a large cardboard box in our front room along with a supply of food, fully intending to install the little trio into an aviary the next day.

Inspecting the box the next day, we found it empty; the three babies had managed to get out and had disappeared. We felt confident that with a good search, we would be able to locate them, maybe under the settee or behind the curtains; they couldn't be far away.

Two hours later we had to give up our search. Of the little owls there was no sign, though it wasn't until the next day that we discovered where they had gone. The three must still be in the room, though we had ignored the obvious place to look, the chimney, so I put down food on the floor of the room and went to bed.

Next day, on entering the room, it was noticed that the food had been taken and that there were sooty footmarks all over the room. The little devils had decided that our chimney was a good place to live and had taken up residence. So it was a case of leaving out food each night for the owls to take which they did, though we never saw them. After about six weeks we noticed that the food was no longer being taken, and we assumed that the owls had moved on, via the chimney, and were able now to fend for themselves.

One little owl would appear each evening on a fence post in the garden or under the security lights where he could catch moths and cockchafers that had flown into the hot bulb. The other two were never seen again and it was some time before we realised where our nightly visitor was spending his daytime hours.

One afternoon our neighbours had a visit from the chimney sweep. I watched the proceedings with our little daughter Emma and told her to watch the brush popping out of the chimney pot.

We watched, fully expecting to see the brush appear first. One can imagine our surprise on seeing a little owl perched on top of the brush appear out of the pot, blinking rapidly in the bright sunlight.

THE MONITOR – FAECES AT THE WINDOW

When I look back, I find it hard to believe the size of the menagerie we had acquired in order to enable us to carry out our school talks. At any one time there was always a selection of tropical insects, such as giant millipedes or spiders, an assortment of frogs and toads, many types of furry mammals, and a very large choice from our birds of prey collection.

The Bosc Monitor was one team member that I was always reluctant to take out to schools, mainly because as large lizards go, this one didn't do much, but when it did do something it did it 'big style'. For instance, when it was angry it would suddenly lose all its sluggishness and like greased lightning, would grab your hand in its backwards-pointing teeth and shake it vigorously, presumably in order to tear off chunks of flesh. At other times it would give you an alarming whack with its tail, which would really sting.

Bosc Monitors also have another vile habit, they don't poo for a month, the story of which I shall now relate.

I had been to an evening talk at a Wirral school, which had been organised by the PTA for raising funds for the school to purchase books and such like. During the talk the monitor had behaved impeccably and as I placed him back in his box before setting out for home, I breathed a sigh of relief that I hadn't been bitten or lashed by the lizard. During the drive home, I could hear the monitor pacing around in his box which was unusual as he normally remained still when travelling.

On arrival home, I proceeded to unload the animals I had taken to school, and put them all to bed, and as I did so I observed my little daughter Emma watching me from the kitchen window. I gave her a wave and she shouted to me to show her one of the animals.

Now as luck would have it, I was just about to unload the monitor so taking him in my hands I walked toward the kitchen window to show him to Emma. I held him up in front of the window in such a way that he was facing Emma, who although she has grown up into a sensible young woman, was at the time a not very sensible little girl. Emma's reaction to the lizard was one of much arm waving, coupled with much shouting of 'Aargh isn't he gross?', which, as you can imagine, alarmed the lizard.

Now, because I had my left hand around the lizard's neck, it was unable to bite me, and as my right hand was holding the back end including the tail, neither could it whack me. So how did it respond to my little daughter's compliments? It did what those school children did to show their appreciation on that freezing morning at a little school in Wales. It crapped excessively, with the offending mess being jetted out onto my face, into my beard, down my neck and in my shoes. The smell was unbelievable, the amount of mess was unbelievable and what I wanted to do to the lizard was unthinkable.

I was brought to my senses by laughter from my daughter and from my wife who now stood at the kitchen window shaking fit to burst, and obviously not able to smell what I could smell, or smell just how I smelt.

When Val did eventually stop laughing and appeared by the door, she realised just what a mess I was in and there and then pushing a couple of bin bags toward me, ordered me to strip off right there, which I did, because believe me, I looked and smelt absolutely revolting.

I had assumed that half an hour in the bath would sort me out but far from it. I had to have at least two changes of water, and to make things worse, my beard, acting in much the same way as a filter or a sieve, had trapped a quantity of the offending foreign matter with the result that I found it nigh impossible to remove. I had to resort to cutting and trimming my beard until eventually the detritus was gone. I was clean once more, but I still stank like a midden.

Having had a beard almost from birth, I obviously never saw the need for after shave lotions and such, but would you believe it, many kind relations would gift me such products for birthdays and Christmas, and as such I had quite a collection; which on this particular evening was a blessing I thought, as I splashed it with abandon over my skin.

By the Monday morning my flesh was beginning to wrinkle from being soaked in too much hot water, and I smelt like the perfume counter in Boots.

As I stood in the Post Office waiting to buy stamps, I noticed people twitching their noses and moving out of the queue, pretending they had forgotten to pick something up from a shelf. I was served in record time and as I left the shop, and only then did I notice the queue begin to reform.

AN EVENING WITH WILLIAM HOBBS

It's an absolute certainty that when one gives a talk to a group of school children, there will inevitably be one child that for whatever reason will always stand out from the rest. Be it through a fantastic brain as was the case with the little four-year-old 'Archaeopteryx' boy, or through sheer fear and horror as was the case of the bilious little Blacon boy.

So when Val told me that the staff in her own school Kinnerton CP wanted me to give an evening talk for the children and their parents, I thought that as most of the children were known to me, and all seemed just normal kids, then they, and their parents would all have a lovely, normal straight forward evening - WRONG!

I had decided that I would take along my four most interesting animals, namely, Miss World the huge Mexican Red Kneed Tarantula, Hissing Sid the Haitian Boa Constrictor, Dusty the Chinchilla, and finally Womble the Barn Owl.

These evening talks were normally split into two halves with two animals being shown during the first half hour; then a toilet, crisps and orange juice break of about ten minutes, before finally, the second half hour session when the two remaining animals were shown.

The whole show would be over within two hours, including stroking time, when each and every child would stroke the owl as they filed out of the hall. I calculated that I could be home by 9.30pm and after bedding down the animals, I could easily be in bed by 10.15pm at the latest.

All these calculations had been made even before my talk had begun, but I hadn't bargained on these calculations being scuppered right from the outset. In fact I hadn't bargained on William Hobbs, and although I'd never met the lad, I had in fact been made aware by Val that William Hobbs was animal mad.

When I give my talks I will occasionally ask the odd relevant question during the presentation of each animal, though preferring to leave the main question and answer session until that animal is safely back in its box and before I introduce the next one.

I began by introducing myself and then proceeded to produce my first specimen from its box. Before the tarantula was on my hand, I was aware of a small arm thrust stiffly into the air directly in front of me. I ignored it for a while but then as it began to wave about, it began to irritate me, so I asked its owner to be patient as there would be ample time for questions later.

Normally this sort of request worked but not on this occasion, as the arm remained in the vertical position and was now being supported at its bicep by the owners other hand. Conceding defeat, I asked the young lad what his question was and gave him an immediate answer, fully expecting the arm to retract, but no, it continued to wave in front of me as before. I was beginning to lose track of what I was saying, having to stop every few seconds to allow this little chap to fire a question - and sensible questions they were too – and then when I returned to the talk I was forgetting where I was up to. I was becoming very exasperated much to the amusement of the staff and parents. Perspiration was pouring off my forehead not because the room was particularly hot, but because of sheer frustration and the feeling that I was unable to get started.

The hand was still waving stiffly and the thought crossed my mind that I was becoming hypnotised by the swaying limb. Stopping once more, I asked the lad his name. 'William Hobbs, Sir' came the reply, followed immediately by another question from this small boy.

So this was William Hobbs. Animal mad, and driving me mad also.

At this point I asked for a volunteer from the audience to come out to hold the big spider, and as a rule I would always pick out someone who has either asked sensible questions or who has impressed me in some other way. I also secretly thought that by allowing young Master Hobbs to hold a spider that was nearly as big as his hand he may calm down and leave me alone to complete the rest of my talk.

William came to the front of the hall and held out his hand whilst I placed the huge hairy creature on to it, and he without flinching continued to bombard me with questions, whilst his mother sitting some rows behind gasped in horror as the spider ascended his arm.

After what seemed an eternity, the spider was put back into its box, William returned to his seat and I then brought out the Boa Constrictor. 'Not a particular large snake', I said to the audience, 'about as long as….'. Oh no! About as long as the arm that once again waved in front of me!

Question after question was fired at me from the young Hobbs, no-one else stood a chance. So when the time came for volunteering to hold the snake, I had already decided that if anyone was going to be constricted that night, it would be none other than William Hobbs.

But even the snake I think, was fed up with Hobbs Junior, hanging loosely around William's neck like an unknotted tie, and so my hopes of silencing the lad through 'accidental' constriction was a non starter.

The next creature to be seen by the audience was Dusty the chinchilla, always a popular subject and although possessing long sharp rodent teeth, was sadly, not a threat to Hobbs the Tormentor.

Finally, we came to Womble, the most beautiful barn owl one ever did see and unbelievably tame with all who stroked her. She had been stroked by probably thousands of school children over the years and had never exhibited any inclination to harm anyone or anything. That is until the moment that I appealed to the audience for a volunteer to stroke her and the inevitable little arm in front of me, signalling its intention of volunteering its owner for the task.

So once again young William made the short walk to the front of the hall in order to stroke the ever-reliable Womble, who wouldn't hurt a fly and who simply adored kids and who never turned up the chance to be stroked.

I hadn't bargained though, on the fact that the oh-so-patient owl had run out of patience whilst waiting in her hot and rapidly-becoming airless box whilst the lad had fired volley after volley of questions at me consequently slowing down the evening. Womble was thoroughly hacked off at having to have her own part of the show cut short as we were running late and as the confident young lad extended his hand in seeming friendship to Womble, her head shot forward in an attempt to peck William Hobbs and no matter how many times William tried, Womble refused to let him stroke her.

Interestingly, as the children filed out of the hall at the end of the evening, Womble allowed each child to gently stroke her, not showing the aggression as she had earlier, not that is, until it was the turn of animal mad William Hobbs. One would have thought he'd had enough of stroking and handling, but no, William wanted his stroke of Womble, especially as he could see that the other children were stroking her without coming to harm.

So once again William's little hand reached out to Womble, who didn't seem to be looking in William's direction. So whether it was as a result of a sixth sense I know not, as all I remember seeing was Womble's head spin around to face the hand of Hobbs and with a loud crack, clout him across the knuckles with her beak causing the lad's hand to rapidly disappear under his opposite armpit.

As I returned Womble to her box for the journey home, I quietly thanked her for exacting revenge on William Hobbs.

One of the parents who attended this talk, gave Val a copy of a video he had made of the proceedings of that evening and on observing the film later, I can categorically state that nothing that I have written about William Hobbs was exaggerated and I shall always treasure this film of what should have been called 'An Evening With William Hobbs'.

ERDDIG HALL - THE EARLY DAYS

Erddig Hall stands on the outskirts of Wrexham and was once the seat of the Yorke family. Bordered upon one side by the village of Marchwiel and on the other side by the mining village of Bersham, the estate and its huge house dominated the area around Wrexham.

Inhabited by many generations of the Yorke family, the house eventually came into the ownership of the last squire of Erddig, Phillip Yorke. A bachelor, a thespian and more than anything else a likeable eccentric, famous for his many sojourns into the town of Wrexham on a penny-farthing bicycle.

Up until I was about nineteen years of age, I had never heard of Squire Yorke, nor indeed Erddig, and it was by mere chance that I became acquainted with the hall and its colourful squire.

I had been dabbling in Falconry for about five years, flying mainly kestrels and sparrow hawks; the only birds commonly available under licence in those days. When one day, a work colleague asked me if I would like to give a home to an injured Saker Falcon which had initially been imported from India and had, suffered an injury one day whilst out flying. The bird had sustained a broken wing, which, due to lack of knowledge in those days by veterinarians, could not be fixed, and although the bird could fly after a fashion, it was useless as a falconry bird.

Me being me jumped at the chance, and I duly collected the bird, a small but beautiful looking creature with a droopy left wing. Each day I would take her out into the fields near my home and throw her into the air forcing her to fly and slowly building up the muscles in the injured wing.

Now it so happened that Val's father had a close friend who was a surveyor for the National Coal Board, whose current project was assessing the damage to Erddig Hall caused by subsidence from the underground workings from the Bersham mine which threatened the very structure of the great house. I was told of cracks in the walls that a man could walk through, sinking floors, leaning walls etc.

I was also told of the eccentric owner Phillip Yorke and his equally eccentric butler Mr Heyhoe and the famous guests, well-known actors who drifted in and out at will.

Our surveyor friend had spoken to Squire Yorke, telling him of my passion for falconry, with the result that I was invited along with my falcon to visit the hall.

My instructions were to go to the small barred window at the front of the house and to tap on the glass, at which point the window would be thrown open to reveal Mr Heyhoe the Butler. I was to state my business and only then would the door to the kitchen be opened and I would be allowed inside.

The big day arrived and as I drove up the long drive, a large pale green Bentley thundered down the drive toward me. As each of us slowed down to pass the other on the rough narrow drive, I recognised the Bentley driver as none other than the actor Charles Lawton of 'Hobsons Choice' fame. He gave me a cheery wave before proceeding down the drive.

On my arrival at the hall I was struck by the sheer dilapidation of the place, weeds grew everywhere, and sure enough, there were huge cracks everywhere in the walls of a once proud house.

Eventually, I located the barred window and somewhat nervously tapped on the glass. Within seconds the window opened and a small grey haired man with sparkling eyes popped his head out, whilst at the same time the most wonderful smell of frying bacon and sausages hit me.

I introduced myself and was instructed by the grey haired little man who introduced himself as Mr Heyhoe the Butler, to go to the side door and he would let me in. On entering what turned out to be the kitchen, I was met by a thick 'fug' of cooking smoke, burning fat and the smell of what turned out to be a breakfast fry-up for the Squire and his guests.

Mr Heyhoe led me through the smoke-laden kitchen to a huge cooking range in front of which stood a small rotund gentleman who looked for all the world like Mr Pickwick, and who, on shaking my hand with his own greasy bacon covered one, introduced himself as Phillip Yorke. This gentleman, with his very thin rimmed national health type spectacles and long-striped apron, looked no more a squire than I looked a ballerina.

Taking my arm, Phillip led me to the corner of the huge kitchen where an old desk stood, stuck a pen in my hand and asked my to sign the visitor's book, which I did. I was then told that I must sign in every time I paid a visit to the hall. When the book signing was over, I was told that I must take breakfast with the other guests of which there were many, all young men and all actors who, when they were not involved in some production or other, lived at the hall.

I was plied with eggs, bacon, sausages, fried bread, all washed down with very strong tea which was well stewed and all of which was eaten in the huge kitchen as the rest of the house was considered to be in too dangerous a condition to use.

After breakfast, Phillip showed me round the safer parts of the house and what a sad sight it was, cracks from floor to ceiling, mould on the walls where damp had entered and the musty smell of a dying house.

Phillip told me that the coal board were assessing the damage with a view to a rescue operation to try to save the house, and many valuable works of art such as paintings and tapestries had already been taken away for safety in order to prevent further deterioration.

The outside of the house fared little better. A huge dilapidated stable block crammed with old veteran and vintage cars, beautiful horse drawn coaches, carriages and phaetons literally piled on top of each other slowly decaying under a thick layer of dust and debris.

The conducted tour over, I flew the falcon for Phillip and his friends and was told that I would be welcome anytime for breakfast and to fly my bird.

Over the next few months, I paid many visits to the hall, sometimes in the mornings, sometimes in the afternoons, but whenever I visited there was always the same routine - the tap on the window, Mr Heyhoe letting me into the kitchen, the inevitable fry-up, even in the afternoon, and the famous guests. I got to meet Charles Lawton again, what a lovely man he was too, and one morning sitting in the corner of the kitchen amid a thick pall of cigarette smoke mixed with fry-up smoke, was none other than the very famous actor Jack Hawkins muttering something about having had a bad night.

My most memorable meeting with a well-known actor came one morning as I was walking across the courtyard to the area where I was about to fly the falcon. I was aware of a large limousine parked nose in to the stable block. The drop down boot lid was open and a very large man was removing a couple of suitcases from the boot. He of course had his back – or to be more precise – his backside to me and so I walked on. Suddenly a large voice boomed out from behind me, 'What are you hoping to catch with that, lad?'. Turning round, I was shocked to see that the large man whose backside I had met a short while before, was my all time hero, a man who I knew, was, as well as being a very famous actor, also a very keen falconer – now standing before me, his huge frame making me feel very small indeed, James Robertson Justice with his powerful actor's voice repeated his question and I remember stammering out some excuse about the falcon being unable to fly properly and that one day I would like a Goshawk.

This imposing character, famous for his role as Sir Lancellotte Spratt, the famous surgeon in the 'Doctor' films, soon put me at ease and told me that he kept peregrine falcons and flew them on his own large estate at Dornoch in Scotland and that I must go up sometime to see them fly. Wow! What a man and what an offer, though I never did take him up on it.

He told me that the only certain way I would get a Goshawk was by becoming a member of the British Falconers Club, who imported a number of these birds each year from Finland and which, for a reasonable cost were available on a first come first served basis to members only.

He gave me an address to contact, should I wish to join, wished me luck and disappeared toward the house. No doubt for a very large breakfast.

I eventually became a member of the British Falconers Club although it was to be some years before I acquired my first Goshawk.

About eighteen months later, I attended an annual meeting of this club in London, which was to be followed by a Falconers' Feast. All the members and guests were seated at a long table and when I looked up from studying the menu, my gaze was met from the opposite side of the table by James Robertson Justice whose first words to me were, 'I see that you took my advice lad, have you ordered a Gos yet?'. I was absolutely stunned that this hugely famous man whom I had spoken to for only a short while many months earlier had remembered me.

We spoke over dinner he, delivering every word with the most enviable diction, me still in awe of this great man who flew Peregrines, stammered my way through the evening. I told him that my ambition was to breed hawks and falcons to which he replied that to his belief it could never be done, but all the same wishing me luck.

At the end of the evening I shook his hand, and he, as on that morning at Erddig invited me to his home to see his Peregrines fly. I said I would love to visit one day, but as I stated earlier, it didn't happen. James died suddenly a few months later as did Squire Yorke. Erddig Hall was taken over by the National Trust and eventually returned to its former glory. It is now a major visitor attraction in Wrexham, with its paintings and tapestries back in their rightful places, the old motor cars and carriages now beautifully restored, standing proudly in the museum that was once the stable block. And I understand also, a very good restaurant in one of the buildings in the courtyard. The big old kitchen is now just a place to be viewed by the paying public – I wonder how many visitors realise that this was the place that produced the first 'all day breakfasts?'.

BOBS AND NEEKA

I'm always up for a challenge and if someone says that something can't be done, I'll at least give it a shot. So when I was told a few years earlier by James Robertson Justice, that in his opinion hawks and falcons could never be bred in captivity, it made me all the more determined to prove him and many others who had the same beliefs, wrong.

My first attempt with kestrels failed miserably. The totally humanised female made a meal out of her wing-injured mate which to me was a huge set back, as birds were so difficult to obtain and when one managed to obtain one under licence, the terms of the licence stressed that the bird must be flown, so therefore to put such a bird in an aviary in order to attempt captive breeding was theoretically infringing the terms of the licence, which could then be revoked with the bird being passed on to someone else.

The only way round this problem was to use casualty birds. Birds with broken wings and such like, which because of their incapacitations, were no longer considered suitable for release.

Such a bird was Bobs, a beautiful adult male kestrel that had been in collision with a car. The driver of which, picked up the bird (which he believed to be dead) popped it into the boot of his car with the intention of feeding it to his ferrets on his return home.

On opening the car boot to remove the 'body', the gentleman was somewhat surprised to find the kestrel scuttling around the boot area, and throwing a cloth over the bird to calm it down, he removed it from the car and put it into an empty rabbit hutch.

The following morning, surprised to see the little bird still alive, the gentleman provided food in the form of some rabbit meat, which he purloined from the ferrets' larder. In fact the kestrel thrived in the hutch for some months and when I eventually heard about it, I decided to pay the man a visit and to see the bird. To cut a long part of this story short, I returned home with the kestrel in a cardboard box. The broken wing which the bird had initially sustained had healed ok, but sadly it had set with the bones overlapping instead of the broken ends butting together, so his future was assured, he would spend the rest of his life in captivity.

Because of his time in the rabbit hutch he had become very tame and would sit on ones hand showing no fear at all. We fitted him with leather jesses and other paraphernalia, and he would spend his days on a block perch in the garden and would be put into the safety of a warm shed at night.

I was keen to find a suitable wife for him with a view to having another shot at breeding, but with everyone who had a female kestrel wanting to hang on to it for flying, I wasn't holding out much hope.

Then one afternoon Val returned home with a magazine called Country Quest, which she'd picked up at our local newsagent, and whilst flicking through it, had noticed an article on the rehabilitation of birds of prey.

This fascinating article told of a gentleman by the name of Nick Faithfull, a retired Lieutenant Colonel who lived in a huge mansion on the Long Mynd in Shropshire, devoting his time to looking after all manner of injured raptors.

Luckily the name of the mansion and also that of the little village where Lt Col Faithfull lived was mentioned in the article. And so I put pen to paper asking Col Faithfull whether he, or anyone he knew, had a permanently injured female kestrel, that they would be willing to donate for my breeding project.

The reply came by return of post though the news was not good, as neither Nick, as he preferred to be called, nor any of his friends could help me out. Nick did however say that gale force winds had been forecast for the next few days and that he often got birds handed in after high winds, mainly through being blown into telephone wires, fences and even tree branches.

I didn't hold out much hope of getting a female kestrel in this way but sure enough, the following day, a telephone call from Nick informed me that such a bird had been handed in – a double fracture of her right wing had been caused through her colliding with something or other and due to this injury she would never fly again.

The following day found me seated in a huge room in a very medieval type mansion, drinking tea with Nick Faithfull, a charming man who lived alone in this huge house. I was then taken outside to see some of the birds which Nick was treating, there were many tawny owls mostly young birds which had been orphaned and brought to Nick by well meaning members of the public, who, not knowing that young tawnies leave the nest whilst still covered in downy fluff, and sit around in hedgerows waiting for their parents to bring food, believe them to be abandoned. All of these owlets were in various stages of rehabilitation which would eventually see them returning to the wild around the mansion.

As well as the tawny owls there were a number of sparrow hawks also awaiting rehab and even a young buzzard, a relatively rare species in the 1970's.

Nick then took me to a huge barn, which contained a large female goshawk which Nick had imported from Finland some twenty-five years previously and which he had used for falconry very successfully. Now too old to hunt for herself, she led a life of luxury in retirement. Goshawks begin life with blue eyes which change to a pale lemon yellow and over the years become deep amber with age, this beautiful old bird had red eyes which resembled red hot coals.

Returning to the house, Nick produced a cardboard box from which he produced a beautiful adult female kestrel which was to become the wife of Bobs. I took her home and called her Neeka.

The aviary, or breeding chamber which I had built was somewhat unusual in that it was made not from wire but from plastic corrugated sheet, which had been painted white. All four sides were of this material, whilst the roof was constructed from wooden battens two inches apart covering the whole of the roof area. The floor was of grass and a few plants and shrubs had been planted, all to aid the natural recycling of the inevitable droppings. In the centre of the grassed area was a square plastic bowl which would suffice as a bathing facility and then there were a number of horizontal perches at different levels, though connected by 'ladders' to enable these two non-flying birds to move about comfortably. Last but not least, a one-foot square nest box, half open at the front was installed high in one corner under a shelter, again made from plastic sheet.

Bobs had already been in this pen for some weeks and was managing to get about with ease, he had also made frequent visits to the nest box in order to store or cache any uneaten food.

I elected to put Neeka straight into the aviary with Bobs so as not to cause her undue stress through keeping her in a box or cage, hoping that she would recover much more quickly after her recent trauma.

So at first light the following day, Neeka was placed into the pen with Bobs and I retired into the attached shed to observe the birds via a window of one-way glass.

Within seconds of the introduction, Bobs began vocalising to Neeka who returned the welcome by clicking or clucking. Bobs quickly ran along his perch and using the ladders made his way to the nest box where he retrieved a piece of food which he had cached earlier, then returning to the perch clucking away to Neeka. At this point Neeka was still on the floor but on seeing and hearing Bobs performance, began to climb the ladders until she was sharing the same perch as Bobs, at this time I vacated the shed and left them to get to know each other.

At the time she was handed in (early March) the breeding season for kestrels was about a month away, although after what she had been through I doubted very much whether raising a family was on her mind. I was surprised therefore to note that the pair became very pally over the ensuing weeks with food regularly being passed by Bobs to his new wife. Then one morning I heard the most unusual squealing coming from the pen. I rushed into the shed and looked through the glass panel fully expecting to see murder being committed. Instead I observed the two birds copulating – was this going to be a first breeding of kestrels in captivity? These copulations occurred some ten to fifteen times daily and in between times Neeka was spending a lot of time in the nest box shuffling about in the mixture of peat and sawdust – obviously scraping a nest.

Eventually it became clear that Neeka was incubating, and after witnessing the many daily copulations I felt that we were in with a chance. Kestrel eggs take from between twenty-eight and thirty-one days to hatch, and on the thirtieth day, I could contain myself no longer. I just had to find out. I entered the aviary and made my way slowly to the nest box. Bobs shouted constantly to me to get out. I peered into the box, Neeka was sitting tightly, I put my hand into the box and beneath her breast at which point she stood up to reveal – absolutely nothing. My disappointment was obvious and I could only conclude that Neeka, after the trauma of being injured had only partly come into breeding condition and had done everything except lay eggs. Within a couple of days Neeka deserted the nest, instinct telling her that incubation was over for this year. I really thought that we were going to be first to breed kestrels but there was always next year.

A few weeks later I read a report that Dr Leonard Hurrell had succeeded in producing a single young kestrel from his own pair of birds.

The following year Neeka obliged by laying eight eggs, an abnormal number for a bird, which normally lays four or five eggs. The amazing thing was, all eight eggs hatched and all eight young were reared without any assistance from myself. Over the next few years, Bobs and Neeka reared many many young, even hatching and rearing young sparrow hawks. A most remarkable pair of birds who taught me a great deal about the ways of captive breeding.

NOBBY AND FLASH

In my previous chapter, I told of my success at being the second person to successfully breed kestrels in captivity, and also the fact that these two injured adults had hatched and reared an abnormally large clutch of eight eggs.

Six of these young birds were passed on to other falconers to fly, though I did decide to hang on to the remaining two youngsters, a male which I called Nobby and a female named Flash.

Nobby was trained quite quickly in the large field at the back of our cottage and became very possessive over what he considered to be 'his' patch. Jane Ratcliffe asked if I would fly Nobby for her in order that she could obtain some photographs for her next book 'Fly High, Run Free' and so I agreed, telling her that I would arrange not just for Nobby to perform, but also one of his brothers who had been trained by one of my friends.

The big day arrived and Jane and her husband Teddy, myself and Phil the guy with the other kestrel, made our way to Nobby's patch for the photo session.

The idea was that Nobby, who was a real high flyer, would be photographed for the aerial shots and the other male for the close up work. Nobby was released first and performed beautifully for Teddy. Next, the other bird was encouraged to fly to a dead branch of an old ash tree in the nearby hedgerow which he did whilst Teddy busily clicked away with his Pentax.

During the time that the other bird was in the tree, Nobby had been floating about the neighbouring fields amusing himself which he often did. But as Phil called his bird down to the fist, Nobby spotted what he considered to be an interloper on his patch and immediately positioned himself for an attack on his unsuspecting brother.

Nobby knocked Phil's bird clean off his fist and with much screaming and chattering, both birds began an aerial dog fight reminiscent of a couple of World War Two fighter planes.

This fight went on for some minutes with each bird attempting to get one over on the other by dive-bombing from a great height only to be foiled when the other bird side slipped out of the way at the last minute.

Both Phil and myself were frantically waving lures about to try to tempt the birds back to us, but the two went higher and higher still squabbling and disappeared over the hill some two miles away.

Teddy, who had by now run out of film after obtaining some wonderful shots of the bickering birds was now frantically scanning the skyline with his 'binos', as Jane called them, and admitted that both birds had gone so high that even his binos couldn't pick them up. Luckily though, he continued to scan the area where he had seen them disappearing.

After some twenty minutes, Teddy shouted that he had a kestrel once again in his sights and it was heading back towards us, though at a great height. Both Phil and I threw out lures and Phil's bird came in from behind us, with Nobby plummeting down from a great height to my lure.

As might be expected, both birds were exhausted but uninjured from their aerial combat and were given a good meal as reward for their performances.

As stated earlier, Nobby regarded this patch as his and would attack without question anything which he considered to be a threat. One morning he bombed a heron which had been fishing a small pit in an adjoining field, chasing it for about half a mile before returning to the lure.

He also caught an adult moorhen which he disturbed in the top of a hedgerow and which on trying to seek refuge in my neighbours kitchen became a victim to his possessiveness, and as if to prove to me that he was a 'real' falconry bird, he even caught a half-grown rabbit, again on his patch.

Flash, Nobby's sister was also a kestrel with attitude, though she never actually chased other creatures, much preferring to sit quietly on her block perch in order to ambush hedge sparrows who sometimes got too close in their search for moulted feathers with which to line their nests. She took many of these small birds, usually on days when she was required to perform at schools or county fairs and fetes.

Ninety-nine percent of kestrels are very poor performers to a swung lure after each stoop flying to the nearest fence-post and certainly not staying airborne like the much larger Lanners, Sakers and Peregrines.

Flash though was different. In fact she was rather boring in flight because she would initially ignore the lure and ascend to a great height, often disappearing into the clouds staying aloft for sometimes half an hour or more. As part of a flying display this was often a disaster, as the audience, thinking that the bird had become lost, would drift away and would not wait to see what happened next.

When Flash had considered that she had kept her audience waiting long enough, she would appear overhead as a tiny speck, and on my throwing out the lure and shouting to her, would put in the most breathtaking vertical corkscrew stoop, falling from the sky at lord knows what speed before pulling out of the dive at the last second as I pulled the lure away. She would then, like a true display falcon, give a super account of herself in lure chasing before being allowed to take the lure in the air. As I said, very few people would see this spectacular finale as they would all have moved away thinking that she had become lost.

Where Flash excelled herself though, was in the classroom or better still in the school hall. And my next tale 'Teacher in a Flap' illustrates this beautifully.

TEACHER IN A FLAP

It's surprising just how many folk are ornitho-phobic- having a fear of birds of many kinds, though most ornitho-phobes say that it is flapping birds that most concern them.

The strange thing is that almost all of these bird-phobic folk will tell you that when they were children they were frightened by a bird flapping its wings in their faces. I find this hard to understand. Was it just one bird that spent its whole life terrorising newborn infants by shuffling its wings before them? The first time I heard this tale, I must admit I was sympathetic to the person telling the tale, but now I find it quite amusing when the same tale is told by all ornitho-phobes.

I myself had a very traumatic experience with a cockerel when I was but four years old, though it didn't have any lasting effect upon me.

My mother, an accomplished performer with a pair of knitting needles and a hank of wool, knitted many of our clothes, and works of art they were too, jumpers, balaclavas, cardigans, even shorts, all with the most wonderful patterns and pictures all painstakingly worked into the finished article.

It was one of these garments which got me into a whole lot of trouble with one of our chickens, a large Rhode Island Red Cockerel who was the ruler of a coop full of twelve hens.

My playing-out clothes consisted of a grey knitted top with no sleeves and a matching pair of knitted shorts. The top had emblazoned across the front a World War Two Biplane in a lighter grey and with the red, white and blue roundels of the Royal Air force on the wings. All my little mates had similar tops to mine mainly because the patterns for these knitted tops were passed from one Mum to the next until the whole street had them, though only my Mum had the patience to knit the accompanying shorts with a tiny spitfire on the left leg.

55

As far as I can remember, no-one else sported a pair of knitted shorts and although they were very comfortable everywhere else they were something of a problem in the leg – mainly because my Mother would sew in a seam into which she would insert a length of what was known as knicker elastic which was invariably tight around my plump little legs, leaving red marks around the tops of my legs which I swear are still there fifty years on. I learned that if I pulled the legs hard enough then the elastic would break at the point where my Mother had stitched the ends together – so allowing me some comfort and also to prevent my legs dropping off due to blood starvation!

I used to go into the chicken run to feed the birds and to collect any eggs from the nest boxes all without any fear of the cockerel nor the hens, until one day when I went in to give the chucks their meal. I hadn't noticed that the broken elastic in the left leg of my shorts had begun to work its way out of the seam with the result that one end of the knicker elastic was dangling from my crotch, dangling temptingly in front of the big Rhode Island Cockerel whose head was on a level with it.

Thinking the offending piece of elastic was a worm or some other kind of juicy grub, the cockerel struck with the accuracy of a bullet, that part of my anatomy which was in line with the elastic. I ran screaming from the coop with the brute of a bird hanging on to my shorts and pecking frantically trying to remove the elastic.

Because I was jumping about, the cockerel was using his feet to try to balance himself, consequently my legs were bleeding from the many scratches, and it was only when my father arrived on the scene that the bird let go and ran back to his hens.

My father, after taking me into the house to be cleaned up by my mother went back to the chicken coop and put an end to the cockerel who obviously could not now be trusted. I was quite sad to see him go, but the following weekend he was served up roasted for Sunday lunch!

After that incident, one would expect me to have had a life long phobia of birds but I don't, although I do loathe elastic in clothes!

Fifty years later I was giving a talk at a local Catholic School and all the children and staff were listening intently as I stood there with Flash the female kestrel on my fist. At a certain point during the proceedings I let Flash fly around the school hall in order to allow the pupils to observe the speed and grace of these little falcons in flight. Suddenly, a movement from the side of the hall where the staff were sitting, caught my eye, a female teacher with a look of total horror on her face was running towards the door, when she tripped over the outstretched feet of a male colleague. But instead of getting back up she crawled the remaining couple of metres to the safety of the door and disappeared outside, at which point Flash wishing to calm the situation took stand on the head of Christ, part of a huge crucifixion statuary at one end of the hall much to the amusement of the children, although by the stern look upon his face, the headmaster was most definitely not amused. Needless to say I was not invited back to that school again.

On speaking to the female teacher who had exited the hall so dramatically, I was told that she had always been frightened of birds because when she was a child ....!!

HERBIE HARRIS THE GOOLIE GRABBER

As a result of my success with the kestrels, Bobs and Neeka, I was approached by John Buckner, treasurer of the Welsh Hawking Club who had imported a young pair of Harris Hawks from the States and asked if I would take the pair and have a shot at breeding from them. John had flown both these birds which had caused something of a sensation as in the wild state in Arizona these birds hunt mainly lizards and snakes. Unlike other hawks, they also hunt in packs or 'pods', consisting mainly of family members each with its own particular task within the pod to bring each hunting session to a satisfactory conclusion.

The two imported birds, Hugo and Harriet, finding snakes and lizards rather thin on the ground in South Wales, acquitted themselves well amongst the rabbits, hares and pheasants, which were more readily available.

Another plastic aviary was constructed and the pair of birds installed therein with, I might add, instant success, three eggs being laid. My instructions from John were to allow Harriet to incubate for a week after the third egg was laid, then to remove the eggs to an incubator in the hope that Harriet would re-lay or re-cycle and produce a further clutch of eggs.

A few days later I entered the aviary for the first time in order to remove Harriet's eggs for incubation. This was the first of probably hundreds of egg removal visits and no matter how many times I carried out this task, it always scared the hell out of me and quite rightly too as Harris's don't give up their eggs easily, and over the years I received quite a few batterings though luckily nothing serious and I believe that these birds could have done me much more harm had they so wished.

The three eggs were duly removed from the nest and put into my incubator, not a modern state of the art computerised, failsafe, guaranteed to hatch even an infertile egg, oh no! This incubator was powered by, wait for it, paraffin – and very clever it was too! I'd hatched some pheasant and chicken eggs in it and now it was being given its chance to shine, so to speak.

The three eggs were placed into the incubator and we crossed our fingers that everything would be ok. This was my first attempt at the artificial incubation of raptor eggs, though this incubator had successfully hatched pheasant and chicken eggs as stated.

After seventeen days of incubation, I removed each egg from the incubator and gently floated them in a bowl of lukewarm water. This was a trick I'd learned from my father when he used to incubate chicken eggs under broody hens. All eggs, which contain a live chick, will wobble and kick when immersed in water, and the three Harris eggs were no exception with much activity being evident. After a few seconds, the eggs were removed from the bowl and gently dried with tissue before being put back into the incubator.

Val and I were thrilled that we had fertile eggs and it was now a case of being patient for another fortnight or so before the due hatch date.

The eggs had to be turned daily by hand in this old fashioned machine unlike the modern incubators, which do the turning for you.

On the thirtieth day of incubation as I was turning the eggs, I noticed that one of them had developed a small star shaped 'chip' indicating that the hatching was imminent. In fact it was another seventy-two hours before the first chick hatched and by the time I had got up, the tiny chick was already dry. I noticed at this time that a second egg had also chipped. That chick also hatched seventy-two hours later. Sadly the third egg failed to hatch – the chick dying in the shell.

For the next five weeks the two chicks were fed every couple of hours on tiny pieces of meat initially, progressing to larger pieces complete with bone in order to provide the calcium necessary for the chicks own bone formation.

Both chicks eventually began feeding themselves and grew rapidly and at eight weeks of age were sexed as two males which was disappointing up to a point as I would have liked to have had at least one of each.

Both young birds completed their feather growth by twelve weeks of age and were ready to begin training. I decided to keep Herbie, the first hatched whilst the second youngster was given to John.

Herbie's training progressed rapidly and he was flying free within a week of his training commencing, though it was quite a few weeks before he had made his first kill.

He had been trying very hard to catch rabbits but they always seemed to reach their burrows the second his long legs and sharp talons reached out for them. One afternoon after two or three vain attempts at rabbit, I was walking back across the fields towards home when I noticed a three quarter grown leveret (young hare) squatting down some yards ahead of me. At the same time Herbie noticed it too and as it left its 'form' and made a dash across the field, Herbie shot off my fist and after a short quick flight, took it in fine style.

I allowed him to eat as much as he wanted which boosted his confidence and took him home. Needless to say, after this success Herbie never looked back and soon began taking rabbits, moorhens and even pheasants.

It was at a Welsh Hawking Club international field meeting at Broome Hall on the Llyn Peninsula that Herbie caught something that even now when I think about it makes my eyes water.

I was, along with a number of other falconers beating some tall rhododendron thickets that contained a number of pheasants. Herbie was high up in the branches of the rhodos, in such a position that should any pheasant flush, then he was in a prime position to spot the bird before making his attack.

A few pheasants were racing about in the thick undergrowth but refusing to flush – aware of the hawk waiting above. Herbie was becoming wound up at being unable to make an attack and was bouncing around above my head in total frustration. I too was becoming frustrated for him;

I also needed to spend a penny. The other beaters could not be seen, as the cover was so dense so I unzipped my trousers and began to spend my money, so to speak. As I 'tinkled' so did Herbie's leg bells, and I realised too late that he had seen my 'lure' and was coming in for a small snack. The pain was excruciating as he made contact and my screams echoed through the woodland bringing all the beaters to see what on earth was going on, and all of them laughing like drains at the sight of me standing there in total agony whilst a hungry Herbie tried to get a meal. Luckily Bob Haddon, one of the other falconers took a rabbit leg from his bag and threw it where Herbie could see it and obviously thinking that he could get much more meat from the leg, he let go of me and flew down for a 'proper meal'.

I was sore for many days after the incident and have since learned that one should never underestimate the eyesight of a hawk. No matter how small the piece of meat may appear, a Harris will always spot it!

NEV

I am always amazed at the intelligence displayed by many animals, some of which seem to understand certain situations and therefore play to the audience; such a creature was Nev. A Harris Hawk which had come from Nevada (hence the name Nev) and although his hunting prowess left much to be desired, he was a people's bird, he loved human company and as such was an ideal prop for my bird of prey talks.

At one of our local schools, I was asked whether, after my talk was over, I could do a five-minute flying display on the school field with Nev. As I find it difficult to say no, I said yes.

During the indoor talk, it became obvious that one little girl of about six years old, liked birds not one bit, and emphasised this fact by sobbing uncontrollably throughout the talk. Whenever Nev roused or shook his feathers, the poor little mite would herself begin to shake, uttering even louder sobs than before. Nev was intrigued by this.

At last, the talk over, the whole school took up position around the school football pitch leaving Nev and I in the centre of the pitch, surrounded on all sides by the pupils who numbered about 250 souls. I assumed the wee girl had opted for an early lunch and had not ventured out with her peers – I certainly couldn't see her amongst the crowd.

I released Nev, who flew rapidly and silently to one of the goal posts at the far end of the pitch, this post was to be the calling-off point for the next few minutes.

Usually, a well trained Harris Hawk is very responsive to the call of his master, and Nev always responded instantly, but when I took a piece of meat from my pocket and held it high on my gloved fist, Nev seemed to be in a dream. In fact he was quickly studying every single child in the group, he then took off from the goal post, but instead of heading in my direction, he instead flew around the outside of the pitch behind the children and was obviously 'on a mission.'

He had flown down one length of the pitch and was coming up the other side when he suddenly spread his tail, which is the same as slamming on one's brakes in a car, and alighted gently on the head of the same little girl who had sobbed her way through the indoor session. I ran over to the little girl who this time was laughing hysterically with this strange feathered hat perched on her head. Nev had his dangerously sharp talons folded up as though he understood that he must not cause any pain to the child. He had obviously been concerned for her and had decided to cure this little girl's phobia himself. How he had spotted her in the crowd I know not, but after being stroked and petted by his new admirer he went on to give a normal display of flying to the school.

I have no doubt that Harris Hawks have an intelligence equal to that of dolphins or even to that of humans, and I never cease to be amazed at their understanding.

BROOME HALL

Broome Hall lies between Criccieth and Pwllheli on the beautiful Llyn Peninsula in North Wales. The house itself was the home farm for the Butlins Holiday camp at Pwllheli and was for many years a thriving farm in its own right.

Built at the top of a three-quarter mile long drive with two pretty little lodge cottages flanking an imposing entrance gate, the run up the drive was in itself a botanist's dream. The whole of the drive during the early spring was a riot of rhododendron and azaleas, camellia and other Himalayan shrubs that had been collected from the wild some one hundred or so years previous.

The Rhodos were not as one would expect, the native-to-Wales Ponticum variety, but some rare beauties with flower heads as big as the head of a man. To add to the effect these acid loving plants were not of the sizes one would find at a garden centre, but thirty to sixty feet tall giants, with huge smooth patterned trunks – a joy to behold. Also, on the boggy area of the drive grew bamboo of all species and sizes and at one point Gunnera, also known as giant rhubarb made that particular area resemble a scene from the film Jurassic Park.

A gravelled parking area outside the mansion was surrounded again by specimen trees of all types. Huge Magnolias, Rhodos and Azaleas of all types and colours, bay trees, a rare spindle tree with psychedelic coloured flowers and fruits, all overseen by on one side, the mansion and on the other a huge blue cedar (Cedrus Atlantica Glauca).

Another huge tree just off the drive was a monster Chilean Pine, also known as the Monkey Puzzle tree. This specimen must have been at least two hundred years old and stood sentinel over the open parkland.

Another strange tree was the cork oak which was to the rear of the house and from which I would often collect strangely distorted hollow branches.

Large stone pots contained beautiful ancient Acers, Palmatum, Purpurea and Dissectum which would have quickened the heart of any Bonsai enthusiast with their gnarled trunks.

Beyond the house lay a Ha Ha, a sunken lawn surrounded by low walls and backed by more Himalayan flowering giants.

Huge Victorian style glass houses had been built to grow grape vines and citrus fruits of many kinds and a huge walled garden had once been used to grow vegetables and fruits of all kinds.

Off another driveway was a complex of huge sheds used in the rearing of thousands of chickens for the holiday camp canteens and there was even a private airfield for Billy Butlin himself to use as he travelled from one 'camp' to another.

When Sir Billy died, his personal assistant Captain Bobby Bond whom I knew through the British Falconers and Welsh Hawking clubs, bought Broome Hall, and as the business side of the estate had been transferred down south, the production of meat, fruit and vegetables also finished. Bobby Bond then used Broome Hall as a base for his sheep business.

Sadly one man on his own couldn't possibly keep a huge house whilst struggling to rear sheep and inevitably the great house, fell somewhat into disrepair and although a housekeeper came in once a week, even she couldn't cope.

Bobby however did have some very successful falconry meetings from Broome Hall with falconers from all over Europe attending these big events.

Bobby used to have lots of ideas on bringing cash into Broome Hall, but very few of them ever got off the ground, and the hall continued to decline.

One idea however was for he and I to hold falconry weekends at the hall for anyone willing to pay the paltry sum of £25 per weekend. The hall had some cottages attached to the estate and falconers would come along each weekend to partake in this pastime.

We reared ducks for the flight ponds, thousands of pheasants for release into the woodland and there were ample wild rabbits for the hawks. Bobby didn't trust people unless he really got to know them and a couple of funny incidents grew out of this mistrust.

One weekend we had a number of falconers from the Midlands over for the weekend and it was my job to take them out along with their birds and ensure that they experienced some good flying.

One morning, Bobby had gone into Pwllheli on business, and I met up with the group of falconers outside the cottage in which they had been staying. We stood outside an adjoining property known as the falconers cottage, which was full of trophies of the chase, deer skin throws on the furniture and stuffed birds aplenty.

One of the Midland falconers had with him a goshawk which, being a goshawk was always on the alert for a meal. Now no-one knew how, but this bird suddenly flew towards the falconers' cottage and entered a room by way of a closed window thereby smashing the glass to smithereens. The falconer was understandably concerned for his bird which, as it turned out, was ok. My concern however was for the broken window, not an ordinary window but a very ornate leaded light type window.

To cut a long story short, the falconers clubbed together with some cash and made their way into Pwllheli to buy some glass in order to affect a repair to the window.

They had been gone a while, when Bobby came back and on seeing the window immediately came to the conclusion that the Welsh Nationalists had been around during the night and had smashed the window. Bobby being English always thought that the Welsh had a problem with his running the hall (which they hadn't) but we could never convince him.

I then explained to Bobby what had happened and (surprise surprise) he didn't believe me, and it was only later when the falconers returned with the glass and did a first class job of fixing the damage, that he accepted the reason although I, knowing Bobby knew he still believed it was the Welsh Nats.

An even funnier story again to do with Bobby's mistrust was instigated by me. I love a practical joke and although I knew Bobby's sense of humour was non-existent, I decided to 'have him!'

For some time, Bobby thought that poachers were taking his pheasants (which they weren't) and I found it difficult to explain to Bobby that his birds were being taken by local fox and polecat populations who treated the estate like a supermarket, and as Bobby didn't have time to carry out thorough predator control these creatures thrived.

At the end of a successful falconry weekend I was just about to set out for home when I saw on the mantelpiece in one of the state rooms two used twelve bore cartridges which Bobby had put there the previous night after shooting a fox from the window of this room. I, unseen by Bobby, pocketed the two empty cases and bidding Bobby farewell until the following weekend, set off in my car down the long winding drive.

I knew that within a very short time, Bobby would walk down the drive to ensure that I had locked the huge gates behind me, which I always did, though as I said earlier, Bobby didn't show much trust in anyone.

Halfway down the long drive, I stopped the car, got out, and removing the two spent cartridge cases from my pocket, dropped them on the drive, before continuing on my way.

On my arrival home a couple of hours later I was met by Val, who said that Bobby had been ringing wanting to speak to me, so I rang him back. 'Hi Bobby, I said. 'Everything ok?'. Bobby's reply was expected. 'Did you see anyone on the drive when you left, the bloody poachers have been here after the pheasants. I found two cartridges on the drive. Did you hear anyone shooting?'.

For many nights afterwards, Bobby patrolled the drive looking for the 'poachers' and I must admit I felt pretty mean not telling him it was a practical joke, but I knew that if I had told him he would never have believed me.

Sadly, worry and overwork overcame Bobby and he died of a heart attack and the hall and park was sold by his relatives for I believe over a million pounds.

The last time I saw the hall, it had been cleaned up. The lodge cottages had been sand blasted; the imposing entrance gates had also been cleaned of the beautiful Virginian creeper that had covered the huge sand block pillars that supported them. In fact it all looked very clinical and it certainly wasn't the Broome Hall that I knew.

HERONS

Val and I were always kept busy with the wild creatures that were brought to us by the likes of the RSPCA, Police, Vets and the public. Many of these creatures had been picked up injured. Some were orphans, in as much as well-meaning folk had, on discovering a baby bird, in their garden and not seeing the parent birds about, have quite incorrectly assumed that the little bird must be an orphan and have promptly whisked it away to be looked after. Some creatures, especially birds of prey had been confiscated from would-be young falconers, who had taken the birds as babies and hand-reared them with the intention of emulating young Billy Casper in the film 'Kes', the story of a young lad in a Lancashire mill town who took a kestrel from a nest.

Where the birds of prey were concerned, we worked closely with the late Jane Ratcliffe and her husband. Jane was the author of two popular books - 'Through the Badger Gate', which dealt with the hand rearing; and subsequent release of orphaned badgers, and her second book 'Fly High, Run free', which dealt mainly with owl rehabilitation. Via Jane, many birds came our way to be rehabilitated, and it's great to realise that many of the buzzards and kestrels living and increasing in our area are descendants of some of those rehabilitated birds.

Another type of bird which we seemed to get more than our fair share, was the heron. Many of these tall gangly birds were picked up under overhead cables and wires, especially after high winds. Others were picked up oiled and some, those that had become a pest on trout farms were shot, quite illegal though as far as I know no-one was ever brought to book regarding the latter category.

Because our property had a stream running through it, it was ideal as far as waterfowl and the like were concerned, the herons being no exception.

The local RSPCA inspector called on Val on morning (I was at work) with a small box, which contained one large heron. The bird had been picked up on an industrial estate where it had been oiled after wading into a small pool that had become contaminated with light machine oil. Lubricating oils cause much distress to birds when feathers come into contact with it. Water birds such as ducks, swans, geese and sea birds of all types, will, once the oil had destroyed the normal waterproofing on the feathers, quickly drown. Those that don't drown, will die either as a result of hypothermia caused by the insulation properties of the feathers breaking down, or far worse, face an agonising death caused by severe internal bleeding having ingested the oil, whilst the birds have been attempting to preen their feathers clean.

The birds had to be painstakingly washed and rinsed over and over again using the weakest and cheapest washing-up liquid one could find.

This particular heron gave Val a good run for her money, when on trying to remove him from the box, he slipped (literally) from her grasp and legged it looking like a bedraggled John Cleese toward the safety of woodland area behind the house. Val gave chase accompanied by the RSPCA inspector, and within a few yards had gained ground on the heron, who, without warning suddenly stopped. Val took off her body warmer, threw it over the heron who speared his beak through the armhole, it then spun round and with his long lance-like bill stabbed Val just above her eye.

Herons being big fish eaters, tend to stab at reflective surfaces, such as the scales of a fish and, making allowances for water-bend, rarely fail to catch their prey. Thankfully, because Val was not in water there was no 'water bending' though the heron obviously still compensated for it, hence the fact that he missed the eye. Since that scary episode we have always made sure that a large cork has been popped onto the heron's beak and secured before handling such a bird.

This heron was eventually cleaned up and put into a pen with some ducks for company. The stream ran through the pen and the idea was that with plenty of soaking and bathing, the heron would eventually regain his waterproofing and could be released.

The pen contained eleven Aylesbury ducks and one drake who were kept solely for their eggs which are rich and make wonderful cakes and omelettes, but because these birds were such prolific layers, there was always a glut of eggs, and so we supplied neighbours and friends with the said duck-fruit. On collecting the eggs each day, I was surprised to see that all but one of the eggs had been laid in the nest box. This is unusual, because ducks prefer to lay in a secure place rather than just drop their eggs anywhere, so although I thought it strange I gave no further thought to this daily occurrence.

Perhaps if I'd counted the eggs on collecting them I might have twigged that instead of eleven eggs from the female ducks each day I was getting a full dozen. Eleven from the box and one from outside the box, and it was only after taking a dozen eggs for a work colleague that I eventually found out what was happening. The man complained to me that one of the duck eggs I'd given to him smelt and tasted like fish, and that he didn't want any more thank you!

The egg-laying, fish-eating heron was moved out of the duck pen to prevent any further mix-ups concerning almost identical looking eggs.

THE BLUE EGG-LAYING, CANNIBALISTIC CHICKENS

Whilst on the subject of eggs, I feel I must mention the strange breed of chickens, which we kept. We had different types, ranging from small Belgian game, to Silkies and Rhode Island crosses, all of whom interbred with each other to produce equally amazing looking fowls.

One breed, the Araucana apart from laying the most beautiful blue eggs as opposed to white or brown eggs produced by normal chickens, was also quite a bizarre looking creature. Of average chicken size, the Araucana was usually, though not always, of a dark red metallic plumage with the hen being of a much duller hue. The hens had no wattles nor combs, and the cockerels, though having only small wattles, would sport either a normal comb or a thick spongy rose comb, which resembled a bright red flower of cauliflower. Even more strangely, both sexes sported long whiskers around their beaks.

Some years before we had acquired these birds, I had read an account by an explorer in New Guinea who had seen a breed of chicken, living around the huts of a tribe of cannibals and this chicken laid the most beautiful blue eggs.

The Araucanas that we kept were allowed to free range across the local fields and we would often see one devouring a frog or mouse that it had caught.

At this time we were feeding our hawks and falcons which lived on perches in the garden, on dead day-old chickens and other forms of meat which the Araucanas, showing no fear whatsoever, would snatch sometimes straight from the beaks of the hawks. It became quickly apparent that these birds preferred to eat things that had drawn breath so to speak, rather than grain and pellets. Could these strange fowl then, be the self-same breed of chicken seen by the explorer, picking up scraps from around the cannibal camp? Scraps of what, I wonder?

THE BONCES

Of all the creatures that have graced us with their presence over the years the most endearing of them all must have been the bonces.

Now before anyone starts thumbing through ornithological treatises, let me explain what a 'bonce' is. I mentioned in a previous chapter how all our poultry interbred, often producing some amazing results.

This story is all about the bonces, namely, Tiny, Tracy, Halifax, and last but not least, John who I shall state at the outset was something of an outcast.

The bonces were, I believe, the result of an accidental mating between Mildred, a little Belgian game hen who was rightfully married to George, and a Silkie cockerel whose name I cannot recall. Having said that, it is possible that it was George who played away with a Silkie hen but whoever was responsible, the results were interesting.

One Summer, I had hatched a large number of bantam eggs in an incubator and had reared the chicks to the stage where they were beginning to feather up and consequently required no heat. I built a large ark to house the chicks and during the daytime they were allowed to go outside on the grass under the ark. This ark had a frame made from wood and was covered in one inch diameter chicken wire to contain the chicks and to stop them from escaping.

One day our little daughter Emma, who was at the time about six years old and her older cousin Joanne were playing in the garden near to the ark containing the growing chicks. Every so often, one would hear a plaintive squeaking coming from the vicinity of the ark and on investigation, it would be found that one little chick, considerably smaller than its brethren, had managed to squeeze through the netting, and of course on finding itself alone on the outside would, instead of squeezing back in, start squeaking in distress in the hope that someone would put it back, when it would repeat the act over again. So it became Emma and Joanne's job on hearing this little chick squeaking to pick it up, give it a quick stroke and to return it to the ark.

Trouble was, the little creature took a liking to being stroked and petted and acted up all the more much to the amusement of the girls. Eventually I was asked by Emma if she could take the little fowl for a walk in the dolly pushchair to which I agreed, at least it brought peace to the garden for a while.

That evening after her bath and just prior to her going to bed, Emma asked whether I could bring the little chick indoors so that she could bid it goodnight. Silly me, duly obliged, and brought the chick indoors for a goodnight kiss from Emma. We should have foreseen the next request from Emma but we hadn't. 'I'm going to call it Tiny. Can Tiny stay in my room tonight? Please, oh please'. How could one refuse! A small plastic cage was dug out of our shed and it was put next to the radiator in Emma's room. 'Tiny' was duly installed; and a piece of cloth put over the cage and so began a lovely relationship between a little girl and a tiny little bantam chick.

Perhaps at this stage I should explain the name 'bonce'. As we all know a bonce is a nickname for the head, and it was the head of this little bird which caused such interest.

The Belgian game bantam in Tiny was obvious although she was much smaller than the normal Belgian, being in size similar to a collared dove but having beautiful 'wheaten' coloured plumage. The silkie side of her breeding was not so apparent. Silkies have multi toes covered in sometimes very stiff feathers. Tiny's feet were normal chicken feet though very dainty and smooth. Silkie bantams have a curious top knot which had developed on the head of the little cross breed chick who as she matured turned into a most beautiful bird.

The interesting thing about Tiny is that through association with Emma, she became imprinted and humanised and not sure whether she was bird or human.

The little bird spent the greater part of each day indoors, but had learned that when she was put out for some fresh air, she could by standing on our front door step and tapping on the glass, attract our attention to let her back in.

Better than any vacuum cleaner, Tiny would vacuum up crumbs after meal times and would roost on the back of the settee whilst waiting for Emma to go to bed, when she would follow Emma up the stairs, step by step and slip under the bed, and squat down to sleep.

When about three or four months old, Tiny came into lay, usually depositing her tiny egg each day on the front doorstep, after frantically tapping away for us to let her in. Then one day, on hearing her tapping I let her in and she immediately headed for the bathroom, jumping onto the soft material covered toilet seat lid and laid an egg there, before jumping down with much clucking and scolding to find her breakfast.

Once or twice, we noticed that there was no egg and we assumed that she'd laid it in an outside nest belonging to another chicken, or as sometimes happens, there was no egg at all, as though the chicken's reproductive system was having a day off.

In reality, Tiny had decided that she would lay her eggs earlier in the day, before she was put out each morning in fact, and had 'built' a nest under Emma's bed which on discovery contained two eggs. I say 'built' because where one expects nests to be built from hay, straw, twigs and grasses, Tiny's nest consisted of none of these things, because they were simply not available in a bedroom. Instead, Tiny had gathered together a number of small plastic toys such as one would find in Christmas crackers and lucky bags and arranged them into a nest. Within a day or two of us discovering the nest and its two eggs, Tiny became broody and began incubating her eggs in earnest. Tiny became obsessed by her nest and took her incubation most seriously, so much so, that she had to be manually lifted from her nest each morning and put outside with much squawking to attend to her toilet, food and water and then within minutes she would be tapping at the door to be let in to get on with the job.

Now because Tiny was humanised, we assumed that her eggs would be infertile, an imprinted bird would never solicit mating from another of its own kind, but obviously on her morning outings, Tiny had been mated, probably against her will and her eggs were almost certainly fertile.

One night, Emma had been in bed about half an hour when we heard her shout that there was a commotion from under her bed. Val and I dashed upstairs and with the aid of a torch, peered beneath the bed to observe Tiny standing next to her nest clucking and pecking at a tiny damp pale yellow chick. We removed the chick which had suffered only superficial injuries and popped it into an incubator to allow it to recover. Interestingly, as soon as the chick was out of sight, Tiny resumed incubation of the remaining egg at which point we all went to bed.

At the ungodly hour of 4.30am the following morning, Emma entered our bedroom with Tiny under her arm and another little beat-up chick in her hand which after a quick check over joined its sibling, now dry and fluffy in the incubator.

We tried on a number of occasions to persuade Tiny to accept the chicks but she would have none of it, so they joined a little group of bantam chicks which we were rearing in a brooder.

At about six weeks of age, the two chicks were transferred to the ark with the rest of the hatchlings and as with their mother before, these two were able, because of their small size, to escape to the outside. Though they didn't wander far, as the chicks on the inside acted like a magnet to the pair and although neither had the sense to re-enter the ark the way they had exited it, they did stay close by, hiding amongst shrubs should one of our cats come on the scene.

The future of these two chicks was decided one wet miserable day when Val and I returned home from a shopping trip, to find both the babies soaked to the skin and obviously close to death. They were immediately taken indoors and placed in the very same cage that their mother had spent her early days in, close to the radiator, where after a couple of worrying hours, they revived.

Emma insisted that they should from then on remain indoors, which they did and were treated just like their mother.

At this point, Emma decided that names must be found for the chicks without delay and in her own inimitable style promptly christened them Tracy and Halifax. Yes, you heard correctly, Tracy and Halifax. How on earth did Emma come up with such names? Well, as stated earlier the two chicks were hatched under Emma's bed on which there was a label stating the words Tracy, which was the name of that particular bed which was made in.....yes, you've guessed it, Halifax. So that's how they got their unusual names.

To make things more confusing, Tracy turned out to be a cockerel which sported the trademark bonce and carried the colours of red and white just like his grandfather, George. Halifax turned out to be a hen and was, like her mother and grandmother of a wheaten colour, though a little darker than them and lacked the bonce of her brother and mother.

Interestingly, Tiny now accepted the two, not as her own chicks, but as two similar chickens in their own little trio.

So now we had three bantams living in the house, the two youngsters copied their mum, vacuuming up crumbs and roosting on the back of the settee each night. Tiny never again roosted under Emma's bed but stayed with the others on the settee against the warm radiator shoulder to shoulder. They spent more time outdoors too, never associating with the other poultry, always sticking together close to the house and in the evening flying up into the branches of a small leylandii tree to await us taking them into the safety of the house before nightfall.

Sadly, we were late collecting them one night and all three were taken by a fox. We were devastated, Emma was inconsolable for some time and try as we might we never did produce any more bonces.

Tiny did however have a brother who superficially resembled George his father, though sporting a bonce, albeit a very poor one. John never became tame and was completely ignored by our other poultry; he was a total outcast who spent the whole of his day running. I don't think we ever saw John walk anywhere, he always seemed to be rushing to find something and one could often hear him, his little feet pounding the path around the house as John, with head held low and neck stretched out ran for all he was worth. Whether he ever found or caught up with what he was chasing we knew not, as he too was to meet his end in the jaws of the fox.

Emma's memories of Tiny, Halifax and Tracy are still as vivid now as they were all those years ago and she still remembers how Tiny used to enjoy being laid flat on her back and would remain there indefinitely, and how Emma taught her to walk a tight rope from a toy rocking chair.

It's probably twenty odd years since we last saw a bonce chicken but recently I accompanied Val, who was looking after a couple of cats for a friend who lives in a local village on the Cheshire border. As we got out of the car we could see some chickens scratching about in the orchard of the house next door to the one we were visiting. On looking over the fence we noticed chickens of all shapes and sizes and colours along with a lone goose. As we stood admiring these lovely birds we noticed one which stood out from the others, half as big again as Tiny and of a much darker colour, there was one outstanding feature though, that made it stand out from all the others – it had a bonce.

A PARROT IN THE GARRET

I suppose the majority of folk would think that the life of a primary school teacher would be pretty mundane, even more so if that teacher was in charge of an infant department, when the highlight of the day would be some small child wetting themselves, falling over, or being sick, or on a really special occasion, doing all three!!

So it must have been a really important occasion when one of the mums who lived nearby came into the school one lunchtime with a small cardboard box, and as all the staff were occupied in preparing for the Christmas concert, it being the last day of term before the Christmas break, they, I suppose quite rightly assumed that the mum was bringing in a Christmas gift for the staff to enjoy. So what, I hear you ask, did the box contain? Perfume? Chocolates? Booze? A clock or some other object for the staff room? No! The lady informed the staff that the parcel was for Mrs Wilkinson, who, being the wife of the 'animal man', would know what to do with the parrot she had caught on her bird table and which now resided in the cardboard box.

With that, Val appeared, and after a quick peep inside the box which revealed a small colourful parakeet, thanked the lady for bringing it in and promised her that she would look after it.

On any other day Val would have phoned me to collect the bird immediately, but as everyone was busy preparing for the soon-to-begin concert, Val decided to put the box containing the parakeet into a store room where she assumed it would be safe until home time.

A short time later, one of the staff entered the store room in order to get some materials to be used in the concert and was startled when she saw that the parrot had managed to free himself from the box and was standing on top of some books in the corner of the store room. The teacher immediately sent for Val to come and catch the bird and to return it to its box, which one would consider to be a simple straightforward operation. So Val, approaching the bird slowly and quietly and no doubt saying daft things to it (as she usually does) attempted to get close enough to the bird to grab it. Something Val said must have offended the bird because it took off and flew around the storeroom looking for a means of escape which at the time seemed impossible.

Kinnerton is a modern school with modern buildings, none of your plastered walls and ceilings – everything was panelled, including the suspended ceiling. The suspended ceiling in the storeroom had in one area, become slightly unsuspended with a small gap where a small square panel had slipped out of place – leaving an exposed area which led into the roof space which carried the wiring for all the electrical wizardry in the classrooms below.

So the parrot, when finding all (except one) escape routes blocked off took the only route to possible freedom left open (literally) to him, and as his little body entered the roof space via the unstopped gap, Val made a lunge, making a grab for the only part of the parakeet which was still visible. There followed a brief scuffle, a squawk or two, and Val emerged from the corner of the store room, her right hand tightly clutching a large number of long blue / green tail feathers which the parrot had shed, as he at last found sanctuary in the huge roof space above the school

'Come in!', came the voice from the headmaster's office, so Val still clutching the bits that had only a short time ago, been attached to the parrot's rear end, gingerly entered the hallowed ground that was Harry Lamb's office, with the news that the other bit of the parrot, the bit that still worked, was now lurking somewhere in the roof space and 'What should we do now?'.

Mr Lamb, who up until this time had thought he was safe in the sanctuary of his office, from the hustle and bustle of the Christmas concert celebrations was now faced with a major dilemma. He was aware that as it was the last working day prior to Christmas, most office workers including those at the Department of Education at Shire Hall in Mold would be celebrating in their offices, the anniversary of the birth of our Lord and nowhere in the religious texts relating to this celebration is a parrot mentioned – an ox, and ass and even a lamb, yes. But a parrot – most definitely not. Picking up his telephone and dialling the number of his superiors at 'the office' Harry must have realised that he was never going to live this one down.

'This is Harry Lamb from Kinnerton CP. Sorry to spoil your celebrations but we've got a parrot in the roof space'. Distant voices on the other end of the line could be heard exclaiming.... - 'Did you hear that? Harry Lamb has got a parrot stuck in the roof space – must have been in the Royal Oak at Dinner Time!'.

'I'm serious', said Harry to the merry voice at Shire Hall, 'there's a ruddy parrot up there. I'm worried it might chew the electrics and burn the school down. We've got a concert here this afternoon, all the parents, governors and councillors will be here, what if it chews through the lighting cables?'.

'Ok Harry', came the voice from Shire Hall, 'we'll try and get someone down to see you shortly. No promises though, everyone has been out celebrating and now they want to finish early, but we'll do our best'.

The school hall at Kinnerton CP was full to capacity with proud mums, dads and grandparents. The school Governors and local councillors had all taken their seats, as before them the nativity scene was about to be re-enacted.

Mary, Joseph and the Baby Jesus, surrounded by oxen, asses, angels and shepherds sat quietly in the stable amongst the bales of hay and straw whilst the school choir sang 'Away in a Manger' as only school children can. Above them over the stable fluttered a huge glitter covered star – a magical scene – though only a handful of people in that school hall were aware that somewhere above the star in the East, somewhere in the roof space was a ruddy parrot.

The choir finished singing 'Away in a Manger' and now everyone waited with baited breath the arrival of the three Kings bearing gifts of gold, frankincense and myrrh. And as Mrs Keith struck up on the piano with 'We Three Kings', in they came – three workmen from Shire Hall bearing not gold, frankincense and myrrh, but torches, toolboxes and a ladder. 'We're looking for a parrot!', said the foreman (who didn't resemble Balthazar one bit). 'We thought it was a wind up, have you really got a parrot up there?'. Mr Lamb, obviously embarrassed at having his nativity rudely interrupted by these three obviously not-very-wise men, ushered the three, still clutching their 'gifts' to the store room from whence the parrot had made his escape.

Luckily the parrot hadn't gone too far into the space and after a few minutes of removing more ceiling panels, the bird was recovered.

That's not baby Jesus!

The parrot, which turned out to be a Golden Mantled, or Eastern Rosella was eventually set up in a cage at home where he lived for a couple of years before being passed on to a parrot breeder who, having a lone female was keen to obtain a mate for her. So the last time we heard of 'Chas' as we'd called him, he was producing baby Rosellas left right and centre.

There is an amusing sequel to this story which I shall now relate to you my readers. Upon the retirement of Harry Lamb, a couple of years later, a big leaving do was arranged at a very posh local hostelry. After the meal and inevitable speeches, six members of the staff of Kinnerton School, dressed in wonderful school made parrot costumes re-enacted the incident, finishing with a poem / recital, which brought the roof down, so to speak.

I have a tendency to write songs and poems about most events, much to the delight and amusement of my family, who will regularly sit and listen to one of my creations, but on this occasion, poetic licence has been awarded to Val and her friend Pam Musto for co-writing the following amusing, "Ode to a Parrot".

ODE TO A PARROT

T'were just a few days before Christmas,
And the school looked merry and bright,
With balloons and holly and mistletoe,
And strains of 'O Silent Night'.

When a member of staff who'll remain nameless,
Went up to th'eadmaster and said,
'A parrots been found in the garden next door,
And I think the poor buggers near dead'.

Now th'eadmaster had always been kind to dumb things,
And being this time of the year,
Said, 'Fetch the poor thing into warmth of the school,
And do all you can then, my dear'.

The poor little thing lay lifeless and cold,
In a shoebox marked 'six and a half G',
And thirty two pairs of eyes looked in,
And voices said, 'Eh Miss, can I see?'.

The kiss of life must have now done some good,
Or was it th'eadmasters whisky?
For giving a flick of his blue and red tail,
He was airborne and looking quite frisky!

A save that would do the M.C.C. proud,
Was attempted but to no avail,
And that damn bird ascended through a hole in the roof,
In full feather, but now minus his tail!

Now up to th'eadmaster this brave lassie went,
Crumpled feathers grasped in her hot palm,
Saying 'Parrots escaped, I hope he'll be safe',
Th'eadmasters reply lacked charm!

'The office will have to be told about this!',
Said the boss, his voice getting angry,
And picking up the phone, rang Mold 2121,
And asked for help, quick and handy.

Now Shire Hall was rocking with gay Christmas spirit,
And parties were given some 'woof',
When a voice at the end broadcast to the rest,
'Harry Lamb's got a parrot in roof!'.

The crackers were pulled and the sherry was flowing,
And prezzies exchanged as is th'abit,
But the question on everyones lips was now –
'Have you heard about Harry's parrot?'.

But help soon arrived in the form of three men,
Not bearing gifts or following star,
For the Nativity Play was now in full swing,
And who were these three from afar?

The parrot was finally caught left of stable,
And securely fastened in pen,
And Mary and Joseph were now left in peace,
As a voice said, 'Who's a pretty boy then?'.